Scott,
Wishing you continued
happiness & success!
God bless!

# WHAT OTHERS ARE SAYING ABOUT
## *STAYING HAPPY, BEING PRODUCTIVE . . .*

"For over 15 years, Dr. Roger Hall has been helping judges and court managers improve professionally and personally with the material in this book. He puts the latest research in easy-to-understand, easy-to-implement terms."

—Margaret R. Allen, Past President, National Association of State Judicial Educators

"*Staying Happy, Being Productive* combines age-old and modern-day practical tips from Hall's professional wisdom as a master psychologist with holistic lifestyle practices, to cultivate joy, love, and success."

—Theresa Nicassio, Ph.D., psychologist, radio host, and author of award-winning *YUM: Plant-Based Recipes for a Gluten-Free Diet*

"Roger takes difficult information and makes it easy to understand and apply. His goal is to help you improve your life so you can improve the lives of others!"

—Doug Brennan, Senior Channel Executive, N.A. Retail – Microsoft Corporation; Board President, Water for Good

"Life can be knocked out of balance in so many ways. Roger Hall gives a simple self-assessment tool for evaluating the *Big 10* factors. He has seen clients make small changes that produce great improvements in happiness and productivity."

—Gary Warner, Director of Research in Computer Forensics, University of Alabama at Birmingham

THE BIG *10* THINGS
SUCCESSFUL PEOPLE DO

# STAYING HAPPY BEING PRODUCTIVE !

## DR. ROGER HALL

*Staying Happy, Being Productive*
*The Big 10 Things Successful People Do*
By Dr. Roger Hall © 2019

Hardcover ISBN: 978-1-61206-185-6
Softcover ISBN: 978-1-61206-186-3
eBook ISBN: 978-1-61206-187-0
Audio Book ISBN: 978-1-61206-188-7

Interior and Cover Design by: Fusion Creative Works, FusionCW.com
Lead Editor: Jennifer Regner

For more information, visit CompassConsultation.com and
DrRogerHall.com

To purchase this book at discounted prices, go to AlohaPublishing.com

Second Printing
Printed in the United States of America

Mine was a happy and productive family. Many of the lessons in this book were modeled by my parents, George and Carol Hall. It is to them that I dedicate this book with love.

# CONTENTS

"All happy families are alike; each unhappy family is unhappy in its own way."

—Leo Tolstoy, *Anna Karenina*

# INTRODUCTION

The habits of health are fundamentally different than the habits of disease and dysfunction. That is why I chose the *Anna Karenina* quote for the beginning of this book. The habits of happy families and happy people are all the same, and few. The habits of unhappy people and unhappy families are all over the map.

I have said these words to many judges. They nod in agreement. Their courtrooms are filled with people who display the endlessly variable habits of disaster.

Don't get me wrong. Successful people do not lead boring lives. Many have exciting, adventurous lives, but they have a set of habits that serves as the base camp for their mountain summits. In this book, I hope to share the 10 areas of life that my successful clients monitor and manage.

## Successful people have a set of habits that serves as the base camp for their mountain summits.

In my over 25 years as a psychologist, many of them working with successful, high-performance people, I've observed what they do in their personal lives—which is the foundation for what makes them successful.

I started out as a clinician and learned all the myriad ways people can mess up their lives. In studying the lives of successful people, I learned that they all seemed to do the same subset of things (habits) consistently in their personal lives. Boring—almost. The habits of disaster are many, while the habits of success are few.

I was a research assistant in graduate school. I was also a university instructor in graduate school. During that time, I learned that I'd grade myself a "C" as a researcher, but an "A" at popularizing other people's research. The problem with many psychologists is that no one can understand what they are talking (or writing) about. I discovered I can take their ideas and make them easier to understand.

The funny thing about psychological research is that academic psychologists get large grants to study stuff and come to conclusions that most of us look at and say, "That's common sense."

Yep, it is. There is nothing earth-shattering in this book—nothing new under the sun. I base my work on two things: old things that have stood the test of time and scientific research. I won't tell you things that are much different than your grandmother told you—because she knew the value of old things. I'm distrustful of fads, just as many wise grandmas are.

When I give advice to my clients, I often hear, "That is easier said than done." Of course it is! I just said it in about 15 seconds, but it will take years to put into practice.

That's what distinguishes successful and unsuccessful people. The successful ones are willing to practice—that's the hard work. The successful people I've watched and learned from monitor each of these 10 areas, assess where they are weak and where they are strong, and then work to manage an area where they are weak—and they work on only one of the 10 at a time. All of them are important, but in order to make new habits, *you need to focus on one at a time.*

These 10 areas are like spokes on a wheel. If one is broken, the wheel doesn't spin well.

One quality of these 10 things is important: **they are all under your control.** Two areas are Exercise Life and Nutritional Life. I don't lump them together to call them "Health Life"—because you don't have control over getting malaria or being hit by a bus—and those things will affect your health. But you are in control of your physical fitness and your nutrition.

Successful people focus on things they can control. They distinguish between a *desire* and a *goal*. I learned this lesson from reading a sex therapy manual (people always pay more attention when I say that). A *desire* is something you want that requires the cooperation of at least one other person. A *goal* is something you want that requires only your effort.

## My One Trick

I teach people to monitor and manage their thinking. This is the first of the 10 areas and the foundation for the other nine. You must learn to identify and modify destructive and inaccurate thinking if you want to improve in any of the other areas.

People say, "I want better results."

Where do better results come from? Better behavior.

They want to change their actions so they can get better results, a better outcome.

Where do those actions and behaviors come from? They come from how you think. Your thinking changes your behavior. Your behavior changes the outcomes in your life.

That's what I do: I teach people to change how they think—to monitor and manage their thinking so they can have more productive lives. It's a simple idea that's difficult to put into practice.

## Focus on One Thing at a Time

I am a professional speaker and consultant. Some people attend my events because it's a way to get out of work. They are hoping it won't be awful.

I know that 90 percent of business education is forgotten within 60 days—by the time the cheese has gone bad in the refrigerator. The only thing people will ask about me is, "Was he any good?" They typically respond, "Well he wasn't so bad." That's the evaluation I'm going to get.

That assessment is frustrating because I'm actually interested in people having a changed life. So education (such as this book) without execution (if you don't apply any of this) is just entertainment. And probably not very good entertainment (you could probably find better).

# "Education without execution is just entertainment."

—Tim Sanders,
author of *Love Is the Killer App*

I present 10 concepts. These 10 areas of your life are important for you to monitor and manage, to improve and prepare yourself for success in your work and life. While you probably have several of these areas under control, several may still need work. However, I want you to ask yourself, "What is one thing I can adopt and apply to my life?" Choose to focus on one at a time.

If you focus on one thing at a time until it becomes habit, you will make progress toward your goals. Focus on too many things at once and you will be distracted and likely will fail.

## What Does Being a Lion Tamer Have to Do With It?

Here's an interesting bit of trivia (it may not be true, but I still tell it because it's a great story).

You can only focus on a certain number of things at a time, and the same is true for animals.

Have you ever seen the lion tamer act at a circus? Why does the lion tamer go in with a whip and a chair?

The whip makes sense—to keep the lions back. Why a chair? That never made any sense to me. (Did you ever notice it's always one of those flimsy ones with a wicker seat? Why?) Because of the four legs: The lion knows what to do with one stick. It bats it away. It doesn't know what to do with four sticks. It becomes paralyzed and easily tamed.

If you divide your attention, you won't be able to accomplish anything. So pick one thing—the one that has the greatest positive impact on your life.

Look for the evaluation at the end of each chapter and the summary at the end of the book to help you choose that one thing.

## One Thing That Worked—A Story

I spoke to a large group of professional people on the East Coast several years ago. Like I often do, I told them to choose *one thing* that they would take action on today. Only then would they be likely to make a change in their lives. About a year later, I was speaking to the same group and a couple of women came up to me. One said, "My name is Maureen (not her real name). You probably don't remember me. I spoke to you last year after your talk." She was right—I talk to lots of people and while I have a pretty good recollection of faces, I couldn't place her. Her friend piped in and said, "You wouldn't remember her because now she looks so different. She's lost 50 pounds." "Wow!" I said. "How did you do it?"

Maureen said she remembered my talk and decided the one thing she would change was her eating habits. After a year and 50 pounds lost, she decided she was ready for the second item on her list. She is a great example of choosing one thing to focus on. Because she did that, she was successful and set the stage to tackle the next thing on her list.

I didn't make Maureen successful. She made herself successful! I gave her an idea. She was the one who implemented it.

Like her, you are the one in charge of your success. I'm presenting ideas—that is the easy part. You will be doing the heavy lifting.

# THOUGHT LIFE

*It's the foundation for everything. If you don't control your patterns of thought, you can't control anything else.*

### It Starts With What's in Your Head

Humans battle cognitive distortions for our entire lives and need to learn how to become mentally disciplined—that is, identifying self-defeating, inaccurate, or limiting thoughts, and creating new thought patterns that empower our happiness and success.

This is the first and most critical thing successful people do. Understand that you can control your thoughts, *if you choose to.* You can redirect your thoughts where you want them to go and create new thought patterns that lead to your success.

I don't teach people how to do Sudoku or to do better on Mensa tests—I don't care about any of that. I spend my work life teaching people how to be mentally disciplined.

This doesn't happen overnight; it's a process. First, monitor what you think. Then, identify those thoughts you want to stop thinking. Finally, replace those unwanted thoughts with a new, more productive thought habit. Monitor, stop, replace. It's a simple concept that requires focused effort to achieve.

My favorite quote about this is Yogi Berra's. He's talking about baseball, but it applies to so many other areas of life:

## "Baseball is 90 percent mental.
## The other half is physical."

He's not so great on math, but excellent on the concept. All great performance in any area of life is first and foremost disciplined thinking.

Your prefrontal cortex (the part of the brain right above your eyes), the complex reasoning part of your brain, limits and controls your emotions. If you have an unpleasant emotion and inappropriate or unproductive behavior, mental discipline is the most reliable way to help you resolve those problems.

## What My Dad Knew

Early in my graduate school career, I went home one Sunday to have dinner with my parents. Getting a graduate degree in psychology, I talked a lot about getting in touch with your feelings (and all of that other stuff—some of it actually useful—that I learned in graduate school).

This particular Sunday evening, I was talking to my dad, who is now a retired professor of agriculture. He spent his career studying soil and agronomy. In our home, we had vacation slides of mountains and beaches and ditches of dirt. My dad would get all hot and bothered about the dirt: "Look at that! Do you see the profile there? There's the A horizon, the B horizon."

So I'm in graduate school for psychology and I say to my dad, "The problem with most people is they are not in touch with their feelings."

My dad, the agriculture guy who grew up on a farm, replies, "Roger, the problem with most people is that they are *too much* in touch with their feelings. If they would think their way through their problems, they would have a better life."

I, being a young punk, thought, "What do you know? You study dirt." (Yes, I *was* that kid.) It turns out the older I get, the smarter my dad gets.

## Thought Monitoring

The first step to controlling your thoughts, that stream of consciousness that is running through your head continuously, is to monitor it. We all have that stream of consciousness, but few people dip a ladle into the stream to determine the contents of the water. Very often, the stream of consciousness is full of trash.

## There's Always a Theme

I work with lots of different kinds of people. Those with the most problems are those who have little self-control and little personal mental discipline. They are impulsive. They create problems for themselves without realizing what they are doing. And it's because they haven't rehearsed patterns of mental discipline.

> **The habits of disaster are many;**
> **the habits of success are few.**

The most reliable way to improve your emotions and to have a productive life is to monitor and manage your thinking. To make that a habit, you have to *practice*. We've all heard that practice makes success. And it's true—success comes from rehearsal. You have to work at it.

## Thought Monitoring: How to Do It

Get a little pad of paper and put it in your pocket—or set up a note-taking app on your phone. Then set a timer (your smartphone is great for this) to go off about every hour.

When the timer goes off, write down the thought that was on the top of your head. Not a long entry, just the most recent thought you had. If the timer goes off and you're thinking, "Man, I'm hungry. I want a cheeseburger," then I want you to write, "Man, I'm hungry. I want a cheeseburger." Or if you just got off the phone with somebody you are mad at, and you think, "That guy is an idiot," write, "That guy is an idiot."

If you do this 10 times a day for a week, you'll have 70 entries in this thought log. This is called *thought monitoring*.

Thought monitoring is the first step. Everyone has a stream of consciousness, but you may not be paying attention to what's in your head. By thought monitoring, you are able to sample your stream of consciousness and start to regularly and habitually monitor how you think. Until you do this, you won't realize how you think. Eventually a theme becomes obvious—for example, it could be excessive guilt or external pressure or anger.

Let's say it's anger. If you've got a theme of anger running through your thoughts, you can discipline those thoughts by changing your thoughts about your anger.

I'll say it again:

# In order to have control over your thoughts, and therefore your emotions, you have to first know your own thought tendencies.

## Thought Stopping and Thought Replacement

Once you know your thoughts and especially the theme or themes of your thoughts, you can do something about them. That is a process with two steps. The second phase of mental discipline is to *stop* the unproductive thoughts. The third phase is to *replace* them with accurate, productive thoughts. But the most important feature of this is the thought-monitoring exercise.

Once you've done that sampling and now that you're really good at monitoring what's in your stream of consciousness, you can work to stop the destructive or negative thoughts. When that anger thought or that anxiety thought or that guilt thought runs through your head, you can think to yourself, "There it is again! I'm going to stop that and replace it (that's the third step) with a more productive, accurate thought."

You can think to yourself, "I'm angry all the time. What can help me get over my anger? Why am I angry?"

Look at your pattern of thinking: "That idiot cut me off." Then you reinterpret it. "Huh, that person must be in a hurry." *Instead of:* "That person is unworthy of love, deserving of punishment, and needs to go to hell." If you can consider another perspective on the situation, then you can combat that anger.

Those 70 observations of your thoughts teach you the habit of self-observation. The habit starts there—a *meta-level* of thinking; that is, thinking about your thinking—followed by interrupting that bad pattern (phase two), followed by replacing it with a more productive pattern (phase three). And that's how you control your thoughts. It's an assignment I give to almost all my clients.

The replacing is difficult, and sometimes you need someone else to help you recognize the unproductive pattern, to help you rehearse a series of different ways. So, talk to a friend. Ask them, what's a different way I can think about this? Find a coach, counselor, trusted family member, pastor—it doesn't really matter other than you need to be comfortable talking to them. So it needs to be someone you trust. Someone who can look at those 70 observations and say, "Here's a different way you can think about it."

But the replacement thought has to be both productive and accurate. It's not going to help, if you're angry all the time, to say unrelated, meaningless things like, "Everybody deserves love." That doesn't help anybody—it's got to be *real*. It's got to be both productive and accurate. If you lie to yourself, and say, "Oh, that just doesn't bother me," well, clearly it does bother you.

It takes practice but once it becomes a habit, thought monitoring can sometimes be "real time" and that's when you can truly improve your success.

I was in Tennessee a while back, driving on an unfamiliar, windy mountain road, and I started to worry because I was driving right next to some cliffs. My adrenaline spiked and I started to get nervous. I began to imagine soaring off the cliff and crashing in a massive fireball (I have an active imagination).

What's that going to do to my driving ability? Nothing but make it worse. I recognized that and began to change my thinking. I told myself: "When was the last time you went off a cliff? You're a good driver. Just stay between the lines. This is a perceptual error. The more you imagine going off the cliff, the more you are going to be distracted from the road. Focus. Settle down. Don't get anxious because it will decrease your performance."

I was able to calm myself down by monitoring how I was thinking. I monitored what was happening in my body. Then I managed it by changing it, telling myself the truth based on evidence, and continued driving on the road.

Many people would say, "Oh, I was on this windy road. I thought I was going to die." They let their minds go, and they don't rein in their thinking.

# You can monitor and manage your thinking with practice and rehearsal.

## The Power of Optimistic Thoughts

Why would you want to be an optimist?

Changing destructive patterns of thinking is an important part of the process of moving toward more productive thinking, but not the only one. What follows are some positive cognitive strategies and how other people think *well*—that is, positively and productively.

Much of this is based on work by a professor named Martin Seligman. I think, a hundred years from now, Martin Seligman will hold the place that Sigmund Freud now holds in psychology, except I think Freud has done some pretty bad things for our understanding of people and I think Seligman is doing good things. He focuses on positive psychology—how we improve our lives by focusing on what is better.

Seligman studies optimism and the importance of optimism. When I say optimism, I am not talking about thoughts of "It's all going to be good, it's going to be wonderful, and you have to think happy thoughts." *I'm talking about telling yourself the truth based on evidence.*

Seligman will argue that he is, himself, a pessimistic guy. There are some advantages to pessimism but there are also disadvantages. There are times when it helps you to be a pessimist and there are times when you will benefit greatly from having some practical hope for the future: optimism.

Whenever I ask an audience, "How many of you would say you are a pessimist?" usually only a couple raise their hands. Then I change the question: "How many of you would say 'I am not a pessimist, I'm a realist?'" Lots more hands go up.

Then I say, "Those of you who raised your hands the second time, I'm going to tell you something you may not like. You know what the difference between a pessimist and a realist is?" Silence in the room.

"Nothing."

What we know about optimism is that optimists are wrong more often than pessimists. Pessimists have a more realistic appraisal of how the world works.

Why would you want to be an optimist, if optimists live in a less realistic world? Here's why: optimists may be wrong more than pessimists, but optimists live longer, healthier, happier lives and tend to have more friends.

Do you want to live a longer, healthier, happier life with more friends or be right more often? Totally your call. Pessimists tend to not have hope for the future and they say, "Why bother?" But optimists tend to view things with hope for the future *and* have a practical strategy for getting there.

## Learning to Be Pessimistic

Can helplessness be learned? You can understand how a person could become pessimistic if they have learned (or believe, for whatever reason) that there's no escape from misery. The trick is to recognize that you can unlearn this pessimism when you feel enabled to change your circumstances.

Let's look at the history of how this whole idea of optimism came about—from Seligman's work with dogs. I like dogs so I don't like this story. But it's a true story, and I'm warning you in advance.

In the 1960s, Martin Seligman demonstrated that he could teach dogs to believe they were helpless. He restrained the dogs and shocked them. Then he put them in an unrestrained situation (called a shuttle box, with a shock plate on one side and a low fence to the other side, away from the shock) and shocked them again—and they would not try to escape. They would lay down on the shock plate and just resign themselves to the pain. If you take a healthy dog and you put it in the shuttle box, the dog will jump over to the other side. No problem. However, a dog that has been restrained has learned there is no escape from the shock, the misery. If you put that dog in a situation where it can escape, it stays there. It doesn't try to escape. The dog has learned to be helpless.

If you give animals, including humans, a punishment from which they cannot escape, they learn that they are helpless. They become apathetic.

For Seligman's dogs, he had to teach the dog it could escape. He actually had to remove the low fence and drag the dogs from the shock plate to the other side of the shuttle box before they learned to escape.

If a person believes there is no escape from a punishing situation, then they will stop trying. Even when there *is* an escape. This is the *learned helplessness* model of depression. Pessimism is the "thought" part of the emotional problem of depression.

## The Helpfulness of the Illusion of Control

When would an illusion of control be useful?

Sometimes, when people succeed in certain areas of life, they will develop an illusion of control, of empowerment. You may think, "Why would that be helpful?" Let me describe an experiment.

Some scientists collected a group of people and showed them a wooden box with a light bulb on it. The experimenters said, "This is a finger tapping exercise. Machinery inside the box will recognize when you get the rhythm of the tap right, and a light will go on. We want you to tap until the light goes on. Go for it." They put people in the room with the box and they began tapping.

In truth, the light would come on randomly and had nothing to do with the finger tapping. The experimenters measured the length of time each person took on this task before they determined there was no benefit for them to continue. Within a couple of minutes, the pessimists quit. They had correctly realized there was no correlation between the finger tapping and the light coming on.

Then there were the optimists with the illusion of control. They kept tapping and would say to themselves, "Oh, I know how this works, I think I've got it." Fifteen minutes later they were still tapping. You may be thinking at this moment, "On what planet is that illusion of control useful?"

I'll tell you: it's *this* planet.

What may appear to be foolishness and even stupidity is in fact a refusal to accept failure—and also an open mind about the source of the solution.

## The Illusion of Control and Chicago O'Hare

I hate the Chicago O'Hare airport. I am so bad at doing my own travel that I actually hired a travel agent to help me and I told her, please, anything but Chicago O'Hare. You can fly me through Atlanta. Detroit, fine. Barcelona? Sure, I'm game. But not Chicago O'Hare.

My feeling is based on experience. Years ago, at the beginning of the cell phone era, I flew into Chicago O'Hare and from there had to make a connecting flight to Grand Rapids, about a three-hour drive from Chicago. My flight was supposed to take off at 6:30 p.m. At five minutes until boarding time, I looked out the window and there was no plane waiting at the gate. I had an eight o'clock appointment the next morning in Grand Rapids. So I got up and stood in line in front of the gate agent. As soon as I got in line (and there were a hundred people waiting for this flight), the gate agent announced, "Flight number blah, blah, blah from Chicago to Grand Rapids has been canceled. Please come to the gate agent for re-ticketing and hotel accommodations. All later flights are sold out and overbooked. We recommend that you get hotel accommodations."

The first person in line says, "I'd like the next flight out." The gate agent says, "That will leave at 8:20 tonight, and you are seventh for standby." The next person was eighth for standby. A young lady in front of me announced, "I can't believe this . . . I have a family reunion I have to get to. What's wrong with you people?" The gate agent looked at me and I said, "I've got to get there. I've got an 8 a.m. appointment." He replied, "You're ninth for standby. I recommend that you get the hotel."

I had to find a way. Of course, everybody in line behind me was getting hotel accommodations. I found a phone book (remember those?) and went to a corner to figure this out. I thought I could rent a car, so I called a few companies. First, Hertz: "Hello. I'd like to rent a car to Grand Rapids. What, you have no car anywhere in the city?" Next, Avis: "Hello. I'd like to rent a car to Grand Rapids. You have no cars in the city? You're kidding." Then, Enterprise. Alamo. Rent-A-Wreck. I called everybody, looking for a rental car.

Meanwhile, the 100 other people on my flight were getting hotel accommodations. At this point, they had already taken their cab ride to the hotel and were eating those warm cookies you get when you check in. I'm still working the phone. I started thinking, "Ok, I just need four wheels. I'll rent a utility van." So I went back through the calls, again with no success. By this time, the whole place had cleared out. I started having this vision that I was going to be riding in the back of a U-Haul with a polka band trying to get to Grand Rapids.

Then I had the brilliant thought, "There are eight of us here waiting to get on the next flight. We all need to get to Grand Rapids. We can rent a limo and divide the cost. It'll be great." So I started calling limo services, but got the same result. At this point the young lady who was in front of me walked back to the gate agent and said, "I want a hotel. This is stupid. I'm not going to wait any more." I thought to myself, *"Yes.* I'm eighth for standby." Still, there's no way I was getting out of Chicago.

An hour and a half went by. The next flight was going to take off in half an hour and I was still eighth for standby. I walked up to the gate agent and as I am walking up, the gate agent left and a new one started his shift. I told him, "This other guy has been telling me all night that I'm not going to get on a plane. Is there any chance I can get a flight out of here tonight?" He said, "Well, let me check," (click click clickity click on his keyboard). And then looking me straight in the face, he said, "I can guarantee you will be on that next flight." Dumbfounded, I said, "But I'm eighth for standby." He said, "Yes, but there are three connecting flights with 25 passengers, all of which are late and none of those people will make the flight. You and about a dozen other people are going to make that flight." Woohoo! *Success!* From out of nowhere.

What activity did I do that got me on the plane? Did any of the phone calls get me on the plane? Nope. Did any of the phone calls get me to Grand Rapids? No. None of the activity had anything to do with my getting to Grand Rapids. I had an illusion of control. I believed that if I kept tapping I was going to get that light to turn on. I knew if I kept trying, I could make it work—and if I quit and left the airport for the night, I was guaranteeing and accepting failure. So what productive purpose did the illusion that my efforts were going to make a difference serve?

This is important: *It kept me in the game long enough so that when something outside of my control changed—when the rules of the game changed—I was available to take advantage of that change.*

If, like other people, I was eating my warm cookie and watching HBO, I would not have had the opportunity to capitalize on the change of circumstances. That's how the illusion of control helps you.

Optimism—the illusion of control—keeps you in the game long enough to capitalize on external changes.

## The Three P's of Pessimism

### Permanence

How else do pessimists and optimists think differently? One is the attribution of *permanence.* When a negative event happens, the pessimist thinks it's permanent.

Let's say I'm out with my friends and we go dancing at a club. In the middle of the evening, one of my friends says to me, "Roger. Go sit down. You are embarrassing yourself and all of us."

If I was a pessimist, I would go sit down with my drink, by myself, and I would say, "I suck at dancing. I've never been any good at dancing. I took Arthur Murray. I took Fred Astaire. I took lessons and even bought the videos and the shoe prints they cut out and put on the floor. I come from a long line of bad dancers. I have a genetic malformation that prevents me from ever dancing well. I will never dance again."

That is a *permanent* attribution to an event. I think I can't dance tonight, therefore I've never been able to dance. I will never be able to dance in the future.

You may do this at your job or school or some other activity. You tell yourself: "I suck at this job. I'm never going to be any good at this job," or "I suck at math. I'll never be any good at math, so why bother," just because you've had a bad day. That's called a *permanence* attribution.

## Pervasiveness

A second pessimistic thought pattern can occur when you make a negative event universal. For example; there I am, sitting by myself at the club, and I start thinking, "Not only am I a bad dancer, I can't read music. I can't play an instrument. I don't really have *any* talent. I'm not much fun at parties. Look at me—I'm sitting here by myself. Last week a dog bit me, and kids in the neighborhood pointed and laughed. I'm a loser! I should go live in a van down by the river." (Thank you, Chris Farley.)

This is taking a specific event and first, expanding it to be a permanent state. Then I expand it to fill the universe. That's called *pervasive* attribution. Pessimists think in this way: "Not only am I bad at this, I'm bad at everything and I'll always be bad at everything." If you fail a math test and tell yourself, "I suck at math," (permanence) you can then double down to pervasiveness by lying to yourself and saying, "I suck at school," or "I'm just not smart."

## Personalization

The third attribution error pessimists make is personalization.

Personalization is when you decide you have your own special black cloud that follows you around and rains on you all day long. Kind of like Eeyore from *Winnie-the-Pooh*.

Do you ever do line racing at the grocery store? You know what line racing is . . . you're in line and you match yourself up with someone three lanes over and watch to see who gets through first. Under your breath, you're saying, "Oh buddy! I'm going to smoke you today." So you get ready. You loosen up. Only one person in front of you, and boom! The gate opens. They put the little marker down on the conveyer belt and you start unloading your stuff.

You're thinking, "I'm going to beat this guy. Life in the fast lane."

Then the person in front of you says to the cashier, "I've got coupons," and they pull out this enormous ball of crumpled-up coupons that the cashier has to unruffle in order to scan. Staring at the ceiling, you hear this as the coupons are scanned:

Bleep.
Bleep.
Bleep.
Bloop. Bloop. Bloop.

Then the cashier says, "This one has expired."

"Oh no! Can you take it anyway?"

Then the cashier gets on the loudspeaker, "We need a manager on register three."

(Internal screaming.)

Once the manager arrives and overrides the expired coupons, you're imagining methods of torture for the person in front of you, and you mutter to yourself: "This only happens to me." And that's when you overhear the last customer in front of you say, "I've got to write a check."

(External screaming.) "Ahhhhhhh! Why does this *always* happen to me?"

That's *personalization*. Like Zeus is on Mount Olympus and has a bucket of lightning bolts with your name on them. He's just waiting until you go to the grocery store. Pessimists tend to personalize when bad things happen. So they attribute *permanence*, *pervasiveness*, and *personalization* when bad things happen.

## How Optimists Are Different

Optimists take the opposite view when bad things happen. It's temporary, specific, and external.

For example, when I dance badly, if I'm an optimist I say, "I'm stinking it up tonight, but I don't have my mojo on. Wait until I get into my groove. Next week it will be better."

In this case, my poor performance is *temporary*.

If I acknowledge that I have poor performance in an area, it's limited. Such as, "I suck at dancing, but I'm good at so many other things. It's okay. Every superhero has a weakness. Superman's is kryptonite. Mine is dancing." My failure is *specific* to an area.

To an optimist, the line racing problem looks more like this:

"I usually go through the lanes fast. It's this person's fault in front of me. In the past, I usually line up with the most competent looking cashier. Next time, I'll need to look more closely at the customer and stay away from the check-writing coupon monsters."

The failure wasn't personal. It was *external*. It's this way of thinking that keeps optimists in the game longer. That's what makes people lead better, happier, healthier, and more productive lives.

It's not that they are clicking their heels and saying, "There's no place like home." They really are disciplining their thoughts so that when they get in the slow lane at the grocery store they're not saying, "Why do I have all the bad luck?" Instead, they're telling themselves, "I should pay attention to the variables that speed up my checkout."

Chances are you're winning your line-racing game about half the time. Sometimes you win. Sometimes you lose. In a random event, you lose about half the time, you win half the time.

If you choose to focus on the wins, your optimism will push you to have even more success.

## Understanding Your Thoughts:
## How Do You Combat Inaccurate Thinking?

Much of our problematic thinking is inaccurate. The trick is to recognize and control the inaccurate thinking that limits our potential and makes us unhappy.

### Albert Ellis and the ABCs

The solution comes from a psychologist named Albert Ellis. As psychologists go, he's very funny. Unfortunately he's dead now, but I'm thankful I had the chance to meet him a couple of times. If you decide to watch a video of him, just be sure you don't watch when young children are around. He cusses like a sailor.

His system for combating inaccurate thinking is the ABCDE method of mental discipline. This is a little academic, but I wanted to include a description of it because you may see some of your own behavior here and this offers a way to address it logically . Here are Albert Ellis's ABCs (with some of my modifications to include a few extra letters):

A = Adversity
B = Belief
C = Consequence (emotional or behavioral)
D = Denial
D = Distraction
D = Deception (self-deception)

D = Disputation (arguing with yourself)

E = Evidence (E can also stand for Examination)

A is for an *Adversity,* a difficult event in your life that you are finding hard to deal with. It can also be called an *Activating Event,* because the same sequence occurs with good things as well. You may think the Adversity, or the Activating event, causes an emotional reaction, causing you to feel bad or sad (this reaction is the *Consequence*—but I'm getting ahead of myself). That's not really true—the *event* never causes the Consequence. Your *Belief* about the Adversity (suppose you were laid off and you Believe it happened because you stink at your job and will never be able to get another one) causes the emotional Consequence. Your emotional Consequence to this Belief can be a barrier to your moving past the Adversity and getting on with your life in a healthy way. That's true whether the Belief is untrue or just unpleasant.

The Ds are about your response to the Adversity and the related Beliefs—*Denial, Distraction, Deception,* and *Disputation.* Only one of these is a healthy approach to dealing with the unpleasant or untrue Consequences of your Beliefs about the Adversity. Denial and Distraction can be very unhealthy if you can't move past them. Distraction can be okay as short-term relief. Deception—actually self-deception—is unhealthy from the get-go and is one of the real barriers to moving past the Adversity. This is where I do a lot of my best work. I help people recognize what isn't true and work to create new Beliefs. The last D, Disputation, is the only long-term solution to moving past the Adversity. You learn to Dispute the untrue Belief (such as the pervasively pessimistic belief that you'll never get another job) or address the unpleasant but true Belief (such as your loved one who passed away is gone from your life) so that you can address them accurately and get on with your life.

In order to Dispute the Beliefs, you need *Evidence*—and sometimes this is found through *Examination (self-reflection).* This process takes time and sometimes assistance from others, but it provides a way for you to overcome the Consequences of your troubling Beliefs and go on to live a happy and successful life. This process provides a framework for dealing with adversity that I have seen work very well.

If you are thinking you need a little more explanation on this process, don't worry, you're not alone. It's another process that's easier said than done. Turn to the Appendix for a concrete example to help you see how it works.

## Final Thoughts on Thought Life

If you want to have an abundant, exceptional life, you have to be mentally disciplined—which is a three-step process:

- Put the ladle into your stream of consciousness to sample what you are thinking.
- Dispute the inaccurate, unproductive thoughts.
- Choose to keep those accurate, productive thoughts that move you in the direction you want to go.

Thought monitoring first, then stopping the inaccurate thoughts, and then deliberately replacing those thoughts with productive ones. This can be a foreign idea if you've never done it, but with practice, it can become a new and powerful habit. And this habit is the cornerstone of creating success in other areas of your life. Ellis's ABC method is a great format for combating inaccurate or irrational thinking. Turn to the Appendix for more detail on the ABC method.

## Thought Life Success Story

I worked with a very successful business owner, Robert (not his real name), who hated confrontation. If you know anything about business, you have to confront people every day—employees on poor work performance, customers with unrealistic expectations, vendors who provide substandard materials. These confrontations don't have to be nasty, but you have to tell people the truth.

Robert hated confrontation so much that he would delay simple meetings or phone calls for weeks. Then he would ruminate the whole time on the myriad of bad possible outcomes until he had an upset stomach.

Earlier I told you about Albert Ellis's model. My client had an Adversity—any kind of confrontation. He had a Belief (based on his inaccurate, ruminative thoughts) that confrontation would end in a yelling match, he'd be fired from the contracting job, and he'd lose his house. The Consequence of that belief was that he felt nervous and upset for weeks.

He was believing a lie—Deception in the ABCDE model. He needed to Dispute that lie with Evidence.

Fortunately for Robert, he had, at a young age, developed a very good habit of taking and keeping notes from every conversation he had, every day. In every conversation I had with him, he'd pull his mechanical pencil out and open his current notebook. He kept this running journal in staple-bound notebooks—the kind your high school English teacher made you write essays in. In fact, he had cupboards full of his old notes. With these notes, he could then gather evidence—evidence that confrontation doesn't always end in heartache, misery, bankruptcy, and death.

For several years, he rehearsed disputing thoughts to fight against his disastrous and deceptive thoughts about confrontation. I tell you this to realize that if you've taken years to develop negative habitual thinking, it will take a long time to correct those thoughts.

**Mental discipline is a lot easier to explain than it is to put in practice. This is hard work. Successful people are willing to do the hard work.**

When we first started working together, it took Robert three weeks of negative emotions, poor sleep, and an upset stomach to get through a confrontation. After his hard work and rehearsal, he was able to whittle that worry time down to a few days. Success comes slowly in overcoming bad mental habits—don't get discouraged. Eventually he went from days to a single day of worry. Then he was able to cut it down to a part of a day.

The single most important thing I think he took from all of our work was the word Evidence. He spent much of his day looking for Evidence of his beliefs. When he couldn't find the Evidence, he'd dispute the negative, unproductive thought. I'm happy to say that his business is thriving, he's healthy, and he has a beautiful, happy family. What more could you want?

## Self-Assessment

How would you rate your thought life?

---

Undisciplined Mess                                    Disciplined

 1       2       3       4       5       6       7       8       9       10

---

Mark this page so you can transfer your score to the summary page at the end of the book.

You can also download the full evaluation of the Big 10 from DrRogerHall.com

*Regularly review how you are doing in all 10 areas. If you monitor them, you can manage them.*

## Steps to Improve Your Thought Life

The first step to improving your thought life is to monitor your thinking. Do the Thought Monitoring exercise as I have described it (See "Thought Monitoring: How to Do It") for one week.

1. Buy a small notepad or set up a note-taking app on your phone.
2. Set an hourly alarm on your phone for 10 hours of each day, for one week.
3. Each time the alarm goes off, write down the thought that was on the top of your head.
4. At the end of the week, review your 70 entries, looking for a pattern.
5. Once you've identified the pattern, come up with several true statements that counteract that negative pattern.
6. Over the next week, and each time you become aware of the negative pattern of thinking, stop it and replace the thought with a more accurate, evidence-based thought.
7. Notice how you feel when you have replaced the inaccurate, destructive thought with a more accurate, positive thought.

Try outlining an Adversity in your life using Ellis's ABC Method. Fill in your Adversity below:

A = Adversity

B = Belief

C = Consequence

D = Denial

D = Distraction

D = Deception

D = Disputation (spend lots of time here)

E = Evidence

# EXERCISE LIFE

*The easiest and least expensive way to improve your emotional life, to feel happier, is to exercise. It will improve your mood as much as an antidepressant with none of the negative side effects.*

Successful people make exercise a priority. When I was starting out in my career, I once had an interesting conversation with a psychiatrist.

We were in a social setting and I asked, "What are you prescribing lately?" In case you were wondering, this isn't really the best conversation starter. He was an old-school psychiatrist, and he plainly replied, "I prescribe exercise." He went on to say, "I don't put anybody on a course of antidepressants until I know they are regularly exercising."

What he said and what I know is that exercise is the most reliable way to improve your mood. If you are unhappy, if you are depressed, exercise will help. If you exercise—and I'm not talking triathlons, but more like a few times a week for 30 minutes to get your heart rate up—it will improve your mood as much as an antidepressant.

# Exercise is as effective as an antidepressant for improving your mood.

Antidepressant therapy is helpful for many people but overall, placebos are about as effective as the antidepressant drugs.[1,2]

The placebo effect, a "fake" treatment (like a sugar pill) that doesn't contain any active ingredients meant to affect your health, actually is real. The placebo effect is when someone's condition improves after taking a placebo simply because they expected it to. This works for pain relief and antibiotic treatments, among others. In each case, the *belief* that you will get better actually *makes* you get better. Your brain changes the chemistry in your body and you actually do get better. No, it's not voodoo.

Exercise has a lot better than a 30 percent effective rate. Almost everyone's mood can be improved by adopting a regular course of exercise.[3]

## Manage Your Mood

Most people's work doesn't involve exercise.

When we were an agricultural nation, everyone did physical exercise as a part of a normal day. We got up in the morning, fed the animals, fixed things, plowed, harvested, and whatever it was we did, it involved physical activity.

Now we sit all day, type, and read a computer screen. We don't exercise and we feel miserable. So we have to create exercise just to make ourselves feel well. When we had more active work—when labor was a part of what we did every day—people felt better.

A study was done of mail carriers and the reported moods among carriers who drove versus those who walked their routes. Those who walked their routes felt better than those who drove. The walking mail carriers also reported having withdrawal on Sunday when they didn't walk their routes. So, if you exercise regularly, even if it is just walking, that kind of activity will improve your mood and make you feel better.

You may have heard about what's called a runner's high. Runners can feel withdrawal symptoms too, when they don't run. Your body becomes accustomed to the production of the feel-good chemicals created when you run. When you stop, you feel miserable. The only thing that will help is to go do the physical activity.

You might say, "Why would I want to exercise if I'm going to get addicted to it?" (There are worse things.) I'm not talking about competitive physical activity. I'm just talking about regular physical activity.

## Exercising is the number one, easiest way to improve your mood and to feel better about life.

If you just go for a walk every night (if you want to go for a run, that's fine too) or if you've got exercise equipment in the home, go do that. You'll feel better.

### Neuro-Nerd Information About Exercise

In the next chapter on Nutritional Life, I'm going to go into a great deal more detail, but I need to explain one more way that exercise helps you. Your brain is constantly growing and repairing—even through adulthood. This is called *neuroplasticity* and *neurogenesis*. Every time you learn a new fact, have a new experience, learn a new skill, etc., etc., you are growing new brain cells or the brain cells you already have are growing new branches—called dendrites.

There are a number of chemicals in the brain that stimulate this growth. They are called *neurotrophins*—"neuro" from the basic building block cell of the brain, the neuron, and "trophin" which comes from the Greek, meaning "to grow." At the time of this writing, there are about six neurotrophins we know about. The one that has gotten the most research is called "brain derived neurotrophic factor," which is a mouthful. Researchers abbreviate it to BDNF, which is also a mouthful. (You're saying it to yourself right now. You agree, don't you?)

Here's how it is related to exercise life. Physical exercise, the kind that makes you sweat, stimulates the release of BDNF.

If you want to be in peak mental condition, thinking clearly, then you need to help your brain grow and repair. Exercise stimulates the release of BDNF, and BDNF helps your brain grow and repair. Therefore, exercise helps you think more clearly and helps you achieve peak mental fitness. More on BDNF in the chapter on Nutritional Life.

## Find a Way to Make It "Stupid Easy"

You can't help but do the right thing if you set it up right. In behavioral psychology, this is called *stimulus control.*

Let me tell you my trick. I used to lie and tell myself that I hated to exercise, and it's just not true. Well, it's mostly true. The real truth is I hate the first five minutes of exercise. At about minute six, I start thinking, "This isn't so bad." And when I am 15 minutes into it, I usually realize, "Okay—I feel good."

What you have to start telling yourself is that the first five minutes will be unpleasant, but after that it will be better. Easier said than done, right? (It is always easier said than done.)

Here's what I did: I've established that I hate to start my exercise, but I love to watch movies. So I set up my exercise and training equipment in the basement where there's no other furniture around, but there is a television. I'll put on a movie and get on my exercise equipment so that I'm doing something while I'm watching the movie. The time seems to go by much faster. And lo and behold, I get to watch a movie (which I like), and I'm working out (which makes me feel better). You can trick yourself into doing these things by changing your physical environment so you can't help but do the right thing.

How did I get this idea? When I was a teenager, I used to skateboard and BMX bike. It was the kind of stuff that was the precursor to what is now the X-Games. (No, I wasn't very good.) We used to ride our bikes in skate parks and off-road. One guy who was really good in the sport was interviewed in one of the magazines I read. The interviewer asked, "How do you get your legs so strong?" His answer was unusual and brilliant. He replied, "I love to watch TV." Of course, there has to be a follow-up question for an answer like that. "How are those things related?" He replied, "I watch about four hours of TV a day. There is only one item of furniture in the room where the TV is, and that is an exercise bike. If I'm watching TV, I'm pedaling." He had stumbled on stimulus control. He changed his environment so he couldn't help but exercise—and that made him a nationally recognized athlete.

Some people hire a personal trainer because that commitment helps. I encourage you to find something you like to do or find a way to make it more enjoyable. Put some effort into setting it up so it will be "stupid easy" to exercise.

## Exercise Life Success Story

I have a very successful coaching client, Dan (not his real name), who, at the time of this writing, has raised $3 billion for his company. His job consists of driving in his car or sitting in an airplane, in order to reach clients where he either sits or stands and talks to them. That's it. He's not lifting trusses to build houses. He's not on horseback, roping cattle. He's not using an axe to chop through the roof of a burning building. Dan is either standing or sitting and talking to people. For variety, he sits at his desk in front of a computer and fills out reports. Clicka clicka clicka click.

Kind of like my job (except for the $3 billion part). Maybe kind of like your job.

How much physical fitness does a guy like that need to do his job? You might be surprised. Every day at about 5 a.m., he either heads to his basement or to the gym to meet with his trainer. Does he do this for his physique? To be honest, partially. But primarily, it is to help his brain be at peak physical performance. His body gets healthy, but he realizes that his body is a handy carrying case for his brain: the part of his body that makes him successful.

Dan has told me that when he isn't working out, he feels like he is thinking slower, not able to solve problems as well. His job—like most of us (including construction workers, cowboys, firefighters, and oil riggers)—is mental. He knows this and feels sharper when he moves his muscles. You will too! (No guarantees on the $3 billion.)

## Self-Assessment

How would you rate your Exercise Life?

---

Not a part of my life            Regular and Vigorous

| 1 | 2 | 3 | 4 | 5 | 6 | 7 | 8 | 9 | 10 |

---

Mark this page so you can transfer your score to the summary page at the end of the book.

You can also download the full evaluation of the Big 10 from DrRogerHall.com

*Regularly review how you are doing in all 10 areas. If you monitor them, you can manage them.*

## Steps to Improve Your Exercise Life

1.  Figure out the kind of exercise you are likely to do on a regular basis—even if the uber-athletes sneer at it. Your goal is to figure out what you will actually do.

2.  Make it "stupid easy." If it is biking, take your bike off the rack in the garage and put it on your porch—so you will grab it and go. Pack a gym bag and throw it in the car, so that no matter the day, you'll always have your workout clothes with you.

3.  Find some people to exercise with. If you like team sports, you have an advantage. The commitment to play basketball or volleyball with a team will keep you at it—even when you don't feel like it.

4.  Start small. Make small changes. Don't think it isn't enough. It is! If you're the fat guy who can only do 10 minutes on the treadmill at the gym before getting winded, you're doing more than the skinny guy laying on the couch. Don't let the uber-athletes sneer at you. And you uber-athletes: Help out the newbies who are learning gym etiquette and equipment. One day, they may be in your shoes—if you help them.

# NUTRITIONAL LIFE

*Your body has a chemical factory that assembles neurotransmitters, among other crucial things, from the food you eat. So nutrition is as much about your mental health as it is about your physical health.*

Many people are more concerned about the gas they put in their cars than they are about the food they eat.

# The food you eat is the fuel for your brain.

You hear everyone talk about healthy bones and healthy muscles. Your brain, which is three to five percent of your body weight, uses 20 percent of the fuel you eat.

You've also probably heard of neurotransmitters like dopamine, serotonin, norepinephrine, and GABA. Where do those neurotransmitters come from (besides a prescription bottle)? They come from the food you eat. When you eat food, your body converts it into what are called *precursors* . . . chemical building blocks your body uses so your brain will function well.

## Fast Food and Pink Tomatoes

If you are having trouble concentrating, if your mood is low, if you are worried or anxious . . . you can change those things by eating better food.

I'm not selling a brand of minerals or supplements and I'm not a nutritionist, but I do know that much of the food we eat has very little nutritional value.

For example: home-grown tomatoes are good, aren't they? How about the tomato on your fast-food hamburger last week? Not so much. Pale pink and tasted like wet cardboard. Why do you suppose that is? Maybe it's because they're not ripe and never can be.

Here's what happens . . . tomatoes are picked while they are green in California and ripened artificially so they have some red color. A mature red tomato from your garden is full of all the nutrients and flavor it should have. The pink commercial thing does not have the nutrients you should be getting. Much food has been stripped of nutrients through processing and industrial production practices. So if you are not making an effort to eat higher quality, nutritionally dense food, you are undernourished.

In general, we're an overfed, undernourished society. We eat plenty of foods that are not necessarily good for us. I'm not going to say avoid this and avoid that. What I am going to say is to get smart about what food you use to fuel your brain.

## Bad Gasoline

I don't have a high-performance car, but there is one brand of gasoline I will never buy because it makes my car go "klonk, klonk, klonk."

It's a car. Yet I'm fussier about fuel than I am about food.

Most of us are fussier about what we put in our machines than what we put in our bodies. So think of the foods you eat as the fuel you put into your body.

## Are you putting high quality fuel in your body? The answer for many of us is "sometimes."

No, I'm not selling vitamins and supplements, but if you aren't taking any, you might want to consider it. Talk to somebody who is smarter than me about that. You will have a more excellent and richer life if you look at nutrition. There is a physician named Daniel Amen, who regularly has specials on PBS and has written a lot of books about how you can improve your thinking and your health just by focusing on nutrition.

### Brain Repair and Terrariums

In the last 15 years, there has been a revolution in our understanding of neurobiology and the role of gut health and our mental and emotional life. In the 1980s and early 1990s, the general consensus was that after the age of 25, your brain stopped growing and started pruning back. Pretty depressing, if you think about it. The only comfort was that when you start, you have billions of neurons in your brain so after the pruning, you'll have plenty left when you die. Woohoo!

Since then, researchers have figured out that the brain grows and repairs itself throughout your lifespan. Sure, your brain is pruning back all the parts you don't use, but then it grows neurons to take their place with different functions. Think of it like this: Did you ever have one of those enclosed glass terrariums in your elementary school classroom? When one plant died, the other plants would grow to fill in the gap.

Your skull is the glass terrarium that encloses the brain. When one part is pruned back, other neurons grow to fill in the space—sometimes with different functions. This knowledge has revolutionized treatment of people with strokes or other brain injuries. (To be candid, some damage can't be filled back in again completely, but the brain is working to repair all the time.) This explains why people born blind seem to have heightened hearing, sense of smell, etc. They do! The reason is that the part of the brain that is usually used for sight gets repurposed for sound, smell, and taste. They have many more neurons being used for sound, smell, and taste than the average person has.

Here's what we have learned in those 15 years: Chemicals have been identified in the brain that are responsible for brain growth and repair. As I mentioned previously, they are called *neurotrophins*. Neuro = the nerve cell that carries information in your brain. Trophin = from the Greek root meaning "to grow."

Researchers have discovered at least six neurotrophins. No doubt, they'll keep finding more in the future. I mentioned BDNF—brain derived neurotrophic factor—in the previous chapter. This one has been studied more than the others, and so far we know the more BDNF your brain can produce, the better able it will be to heal and grow throughout your lifespan. Right now, you're about to get on Amazon and see if they sell bottles of BDNF, aren't you? They sell stuff that may help, but there are ways you can boost BDNF by what you eat.

**Curry.** I love Indian food. As a kid I lived in India and developed a taste for curry. One of the key ingredients in most curries is turmeric, and its active component is curcumin. It gives curries their yellow color. You may have heard of the anti-inflammatory properties of curcumin and turmeric, but you may not know that it has also been shown to boost the production of BDNF. You may be one of those people who doesn't like curry and the thought of a plate of matar paneer sounds awful to you—and if that's you, there are alternatives to eating curry every day. You can buy turmeric supplements or curcumin supplements. Of course, I'm not giving you specific medical or nutritional advice. Talk to a nutritionist about what might work best for you.

**Niacin.** Niacin is also known as B3, one of the B complex vitamins. It has been shown to increase the production of BDNF. All the B complex vitamins are good for your brain and may help in memory consolidation.

I had a client, years and years ago, who was a self-admitted drunk. He was proud that he had never experienced a blackout (an alcohol-induced period of amnesia). He was absolutely convinced that it was because he ate B vitamins like Tic-Tacs. I don't recommend that you follow his advice, but I do know B vitamins are good for your brain, and particularly niacin for the production of BDNF.

**Fish oil.** The research about fish oil is solid: it helps boost BDNF. Even if you don't care about BDNF, tons of research results also show that fish oil is good for pretty much every emotional disturbance. I was at a continuing education class years ago put on by a professor, Dr. Nick Hall (no relation to me), on nutritional interventions for mental health. As he scrolled through almost every category of mental illness, he said, "and fish oil." At one point toward the end of the day, he said, "I know you are getting tired of hearing about fish oil, but it seems to be good for the treatment of almost every mental illness."

**Fermented Foods**. You've seen Jamie Lee Curtis pitch a brand of yogurt. The claims have been about improving your digestion. What wasn't well known when she started those commercials was the relationship between fermented foods and brain health. It isn't just yogurt or even the brand of yogurt she sold, it is almost any fermented food with live, active cultures. Here's where I always get this question, "So you mean beer?" I'm afraid not. I'm talking about foods that are fermented with bacteria, not yeast. (A big "I'm sorry" to the entire state of Wisconsin.) I'm talking about things like yogurt, kefir, sauerkraut, kimchee, kombucha, and pickles (the kind on the refrigerated aisle). They are all shown to increase the production of BDNF.

## Gut Health and Brain Health

Here is where we need to start talking about gut health. What we've learned in the last 15 years from research by gastroenterologists is human beings are symbiotic with the bazillions of bacteria that live in our digestive systems.

If you don't count blood cells, 90 percent of the cells in our bodies are not human. They are bacteria.

You may be thinking that bacteria are bad. Yes, there are bad-guy bacteria. But in our bodies, we need the good-guy bacteria. We used to think our digestion was largely a chemical (acid) and mechanical (stomach contractions) process. What researchers have discovered is that we are almost entirely dependent on the bacteria in our guts to digest our food. Further, and more important for my work, those bacteria communicate directly to our nervous system through the lining of our intestines to the *vagus nerve*. The vagus nerve is the longest nerve fiber in your body and is an eight-lane super-highway with 90 percent of the traffic heading north to the brain.

Those bacteria in your gut not only send signals to your brain through the intestinal wall, they are in the business of creating neurotransmitters. You've heard of serotonin, which regulates your mood. You think you can get that in a pill. Ninety percent of the serotonin in your body is in your digestive system, not your brain. In fact, while much of it is manufactured in your brain, a chunk of it is manufactured by those bacteria in your gut. Another neurotransmitter, GABA (gamma-aminobutyric acid), is also manufactured by those bacteria. GABA is your body's natural Valium. It does much more than reduce anxiety, but one of its jobs is to calm you down.

There is a war going on in your gut. In your gut, there are the good-guy bacteria and the bad-guy bacteria. They are always at war. There are dozens of ways we kill off the good-guy bacteria and allow the bad-guy bacteria the win. Much of it is the kinds of foods we eat or some of the medicines we take (namely, excessive use of antibiotics). If we change our food intake to feed the good-guy bacteria, they win the war.

Without going into the dozens of controlled research projects (both animal model and human experiments), the outcomes are pretty clear. When the good-guy bacteria are winning the war, humans and animals feel better, have less anxiety, and think better.

If you are interested in learning more, I'd recommend a couple books on the topic: *The Mind-Gut Connection* by Emeran Mayer (Harper Wave, reprint edition, 2018) and *Brain Maker* by David Perlmutter and Kristin Loberg (Little, Brown and Company, 2015).

## Nutritional Life Success Story

For some reason, we love to associate Rock and Roll with decadent lifestyles, drug-fueled performances, and tragic early deaths. Sure, we all know the stories. It is a hard life to be a musician on the road (listen closely to Bob Seeger's song *Turn the Page* to get a glimpse of the strain). Sure, lots of famous musicians turn to cocaine to keep up their energy or opiates to help them calm down after a show. And many have gritty autobiographies about how they got clean.

These musicians are high-performance people who need to be at the top of their game to put on a show. Recently, I got to go back stage at a couple of concerts—bands you've heard of and whose music you've listened to on the radio, in the airport, in movies. A couple of my friends have behind-the-scenes jobs that take them to the dark tunnels and crowded, ratty offices under dozens of arenas in the country. You might think that the booze was flowing, every flat surface was covered by lines of cocaine, and semi-naked women were wandering from dressing room to dressing room.

You couldn't be farther from the truth.

Between sets, guitarists were calling their families to say goodnight to their kids and wives. One band member runs for an hour on the treadmill before the show to get himself in the zone for the concert.

I got a chance to eat dinner with each of my friends on those two nights. Each band had hired caterers with contractually defined food choices. All were healthy. I got to choose from a better selection of foods those two nights than I ever would have in most chain restaurants. In one case, my friend special-ordered a spaghetti squash for the lead singer. When the singer got his spaghetti squash in the Styrofoam clamshell, you'd think he hit the lottery. He was oohing and ahhing about the meal he was going to eat (this just after the crowd was giving him a standing ovation).

He knew, and lots of high-performance people know, that in order to do their jobs well, they need to put good fuel in their systems. If you want to learn more about rock and rollers and healthy lifestyles, read *How to Be a Man: (and Other Illusions)* by Duff McKagan, the bass player for the original lineup of Guns N' Roses and Velvet Revolver (co-author Chris Kornelis, Da Capo Press, 2015).

## Self-Assessment

How would you rate your Nutritional Life?

---

Not a part of my life                        Focused and Deliberate

| 1 | 2 | 3 | 4 | 5 | 6 | 7 | 8 | 9 | 10 |

---

Mark this page so you can transfer your score to the summary page at the end of the book.

You can also download the full evaluation of the Big 10 from DrRogerHall.com

*Regularly review how you are doing in all 10 areas. If you monitor them, you can manage them.*

## Steps to Improve Your Nutritional Life

1. Start sampling fermented foods. Find the ones you enjoy eating and the ones that agree with your system. Sometimes, your digestive system will act badly when you begin to eat fermented foods—because the bad-guy bacteria have been winning the war and you've sent in replacement troops to fight them. Give it time and experiment with different fermented foods.

2. Find a nutritionist or dietician who is knowledgeable about the mind-gut connection. Make small changes in the food you are eating. Remember, single small changes are far more likely to be maintained than changing your diet all together.

3. Read up on the relationship between nutrition and your brain (I've suggested a few options).

4. Try foods you have never tried. Sometimes, a variety of foods will help you in ways your old tried and true favorites won't. Experiment a little. You might even find some new favorites!

# LOVE LIFE

*If you have trouble at home, you're going to have trouble at work. If you're having trouble at work, you're going to have trouble at home.*

I had a sex therapy professor who used to say (by the way, I've found that people tend to pay more attention when I start *any* sentence this way), "If you're having trouble in the bedroom, you're going to have trouble in the kitchen. If you're having trouble in the kitchen, you're going to have trouble in the bedroom." His point was this: We are integrated creatures. Problems in one area create problems in other areas. I expand his definition to say, "If you're having trouble at home, you're going to have trouble at work. If you're having trouble at work, you're going to have trouble at home."

When you hear "love life," you may be thinking about sex or romantic relationships. That is part of it, *but certainly not all of it.* When I'm talking about love life, I mean your primary love relationship—your spouse or your partner. But I also mean more than that. I love my parents, I love my sister, I love my children. It's not all romantic love, but it is love. Romantic love and marital relationships are a big part of love life, but I'm talking about the importance of all love relationships in your family.

If there's trouble at home—whether it's with a spouse, sibling, parent, or child, it will affect your life, your happiness, and your ability to succeed and focus on what brings you success.

Many of the successful families I know have one black sheep, some squirrelly kid who hasn't turned out well. That's the broken spoke in their whole family wheel. They've got to fix that if they want to be able to look back on their lives with no regrets. That squirrelly kid takes up a tremendous amount of their mental energy and prevents them from being at the top of their game in the other nine areas of a successful life.

Many books have been written on parenting and I'm not going to attempt to address the topic in depth, but here's what I know in a nutshell: Great parenting is about teaching your kid how to wait.

The master skill is the delay of gratification—or *willpower*. By the time your kid is 12, the cow is out of the barn. Early childhood is super important.

## The primary lesson to teach a child is self-control —the delay of gratification.

Teach a kid that and they're head and shoulders above everybody else. One way to destroy a kid is to bow down at the idol of your child.

Unfortunately, we have a culture that idolizes children. "Never say 'no' to your child because they hear 'no' too often." No, they don't. Success in life is dependent, more than any other factor, on the *delay of gratification*. The word "no" is the most important word in learning the delay of gratification. If you want to read more about the topic, read *Willpower: Rediscovering the Greatest Human Strength* by Roy F. Baumeister and John Tierney. It reads like a novel.

If you're worried about your kid being in jail, you won't be able to concentrate enough to be successful in any other area of your life. If you've just finished a three-hour argument with your spouse, you're going to be worthless the rest of the day. Trouble at home, trouble at work. Trouble at work, trouble at home.

### If Mama Ain't Happy . . .

"If Mama ain't happy, ain't nobody happy." "Happy wife, happy life."

People tell me over and over again, "I want to have better performance at work, but I don't really want to talk about my family life."

In my work in leadership development, I've come to know and understand that invariably, problems at home will creep into problems at work.

# If you don't get your home life right, you're going to have trouble in your work and in every other area of your life.

You may think that work and home are completely separate. But if you had an argument with your spouse before work, once you get to work are you going to be able to turn that off? No. So it's important that you have a good love life. Not only that, you need to have healthy home and family relationships, which can lead to a productive life everywhere.

## The Dirty Little Secret of Marital Communication

In the United States, 40-50 percent of marriages end in divorce. For second marriages, the divorce rate is 60 percent. For third marriages, it's 73 percent. This means the divorce rate amps up if you didn't fix the problem in your relationship to begin with.[4]

There are a lot of good resources out there to help improve your love life, including a guy named John Gottman. Gottman was interested in studying marital communication and wrote several books on the topic. I'd argue he's the leading thinker in this area.

We used to believe that marital communication was like what you see people do in communication skills training. For example, sometimes it went like this, "What I hear you saying is . . . " which is referred to as the "I statement." Plus the "feeling" words—"I feel hurt when you criticize my mother."

In my graduate school internship, I was part of a research study on marital communication where we gave people pens and told them that whoever has the pen has the power. The first person would say something like, "I feel hurt when you criticize my mother." Then they would hand the pen over to their spouse. "So you feel hurt when I criticize your mother. Did I get that right?" Hand the pen back, "Yes, but I don't think you understood how much it hurt me. It really hurts me a lot and I get mad at you." (Exchange the pen.) "So you get mad at me when I criticize your mother and that hurts and . . ."

We used to think that's the way healthy couples communicated. The dirty little secret is that, in reality, healthy couples don't communicate like that at all.

Do you want to know who communicates that way? Therapy graduates and people who have gone to mandatory sensitivity training communicate that way. Real people don't talk like that.

John Gottman did research to determine how real, healthy couples communicate. Guess what? It's all in the nickel-and-dime communication.

## The Love Lab

Gottman got a research grant, and with it he got a bed and breakfast in Seattle overlooking the Puget Sound. He and his research team told newlyweds, "You can come to our bed and breakfast and stay for free, provided you let us videotape and audiotape you in every room of the house except for the bedroom and the bathroom. Oh, and you have to wear a heart rate monitor and a blood pressure monitor. But besides that, the place is yours. Have fun!"

The answer I would have given is not "No," it would have been "Hell no!" But lo and behold, couples signed up.

What Gottman thought he was going to hear were what I call "John and Marcia" conversations: "Oh John, I'll hold you in my heart forever," and "Oh Marcia, I will love you until the end of time . . ."

In actuality, what he got was very different.

The conversations went something like this instead:

"Oh look at that boat over there. Do you want to buy a sailboat?"

"I don't know. Sailing doesn't sound like that much fun. Seems like a lot of work."

"Yeah, but on a nice day like today that would be fun."

"Yeah, but we live in Seattle and it rains all the time."

He captured them reading the newspaper too.

"Do you get *The Far Side?* I think that guy is twisted."

"I think he's funny."

So Gottman, after going over the recordings, realized he had thousands of hours of couples talking like that and he was thinking "I've got nothing but junk data." Then one of his graduate students said, "Gee, Dr. Gottman, what if that is the way healthy couples communicate?" (She gets a footnote, he got the Gottman Institute—welcome to the world of graduate school.)

## How Happy Couples Talk

So Gottman and his students went back through and re-analyzed the videos. They found that healthy couples don't communicate with the "John and Marcia" and "What I hear you saying is . . ." kind of conversations.

This is how they communicate: they make a bid (a bid for intimacy) and it's not asking for sex, it's simply a conversation starter. It's a small-talk conversation starter.

The most important thing Gottman found was that healthy communication among couples starts with the *nickel-and-dime small talk.*

A lot of you may be thinking "Oh I hate small talk. It's so superficial." Actually, small talk is very important because you realize who is crazy, who is nasty, and who you don't want to be around. There you are at the bus stop and you say, "Nice weather we're having today," to the guy standing next to you. He responds with, "Yeah, but you can't trust it to last. Ever since Dick Cheney unleashed the Haliburton Weather machine, the government has been controlling the weather to control our lives." At this point, your small talk conversation starter has served its purpose. You quickly reach into your pocket and pretend to answer your phone. You slowly, slowly move away from the crazy man.

What we know about good relationships is they are all built on small talk. Gottman found that there is a bid for small talk—a conversation starter—and three different types of responses (which he calls "turns") to that bid. Let's demonstrate the three types of turns to a bid.

## Bid and Turn 1

Brian: "How are you?"

Roger: "I'm fine. I'm having a really good day."

The bid was, "How are you?" and the turn was, "I'm fine. I'm having a really good day." That's what's called a *turning toward* response. Now what I didn't say was, "Brian, thank you for asking. It really makes me feel cared for and loved." (Because that would be creepy and Brian would start to look at his phone and slowly move away.) I said, "I'm fine. I'm having a really good day." It was mildly positive and on topic. Those are the two most important aspects of the turning toward. *Mildly positive* and *on topic*.

## Bid and Turn 2

Brian: "How are you?"

Roger: "What are you so nosey for? Don't get into my space."

This response is called the *turning against*. This is *on topic* but it's *negative*.

## Bid and Turn 3

Brian: "How are you?"

Roger: "Wait a minute. Let me check this." (Looks at phone.) "I'm sorry . . . what were you saying?"

This is *turning away*. It's neither positive nor negative, but it is *off topic*.

What Gottman found is that healthy couples predominantly made *turning toward* responses to bids.

### The Seven-Year Itch

What Gottman found is that couples who divorce somewhere between year five and year nine of their marriage, which he calls the seven-year itch, tended to predominately have *turning away* responses to bids.

He also found that people who divorce at what he calls the 14-year itch had a preponderance of the *turning against* communication.

So the seven-year itch marital poison is turning away. It's when couples are sort of running parallel to one another and not really talking.

Right now you might be questioning, "What you're telling me is that couples that are angry with each other and in conflict last longer than those who don't?"

Exactly, because at least they have a relationship. Yes, it's a bad relationship, but at least they're interacting.

A surprising conclusion from this study was that unhappy couples last longer than apathetic couples. That's why *turning away* is marital poison. Turning against is also bad, but what Gottman found is that it doesn't always matter. As long as you have plenty of turning toward conversations, you can counteract the turning against.

In other words, the secret sauce is not the amount of negative communication in a relationship—*it's the preponderance of your turning toward* communication. If you have a lot of positive small talk and still fight, yes you'd be that off-again, on-again couple—"I hate you and I want to kill you with a knife," and "I'm sorry, baby. I shouldn't have said that. I love you so much." (I'm exaggerating here.) Nevertheless, you can be a passionate couple where you're doing a lot of turning toward and turning against, but if you have a preponderance of the turning toward, your marriage is likely to last. *Because it's the amount of positive communication, not the amount of negative communication in a relationship, that makes it a lasting one.*

The secret to having a great marriage is not about fighting fair. It's not about *not* fighting. What I want to know is, "Do you have a lot of *turning toward* in your communication?" because that is what predicts marital success. Turning toward isn't the John and Marcia conversation. It is John and Marcia paying attention to the nickel-and-dime conversations they have.

## Predictors of Marital Success

Some other Gottman secrets:

The number one predictor of marital success is the husband's willingness to cooperate with the wife.

Men, if you learn how to say, "Sure thing, honey," that will be your first predictor of a successful marriage.

The number two predictor of marital success is the wife's ability to give light-hearted feedback to hard things. It's her ability to "honey talk" her husband.

For women, if you believe the men in your lives need to talk face to face about problems, understand that men don't want to do that. If you do that, men feel like they're going to die.

If men want to tell someone they're an idiot, how do they do it? Do they say, "I have a problem with you and I think we need to talk . . . "? No—men rarely do that. Men say, in a joking way, "You numbskull. What are you thinking?" We joke. We tease and make fun of each other.

Ladies, most men cannot handle a face-to-face, eye-to-eye conversation about a problem. It's different for women—all you need is two cups of coffee and a small table and you can talk it through. Men need another activity to do that gives us an "out." This is why men love golf, because we can have a conversation on a deep topic, but there's always a way to change the topic. If the conversation gets too intense, we start talking about slicing and hooking.

## Men Versus Women Talking:
## Face to Face Versus Side by Side

Imagine a couple of guys working on a carburetor, and one of them says, "Let it out a little bit more. Can you give me the number two Phillips for this?" As he's letting it idle he says, "Does your wife ever . . . (fill in the blank)?"

As men, we need an activity to do because if the other guy starts to get too intense, we can shift the topic back onto the activity. Men need something else they can talk about—a conversation escape route—otherwise they will do what's referred to as "flooding."

Because of testosterone plus adrenaline, if men get emotionally too intense, they "flood out." It's like when a car with too much gasoline floods and won't start. This happens with confrontational conversations that lead to something like, "Why won't you talk to me? Please talk to me." He's flooded. No, he's not drunk. He's just flooded. Men, you know this because once you reach a certain point, the engine is flooded and you shut down. Guys get overwhelmed.

Here's where honey talk comes in. A woman's ability to honey talk a man (some of you ladies are murmuring to yourselves, "That's demeaning!") makes all the difference when you need to give some tough feedback. Maybe it seems demeaning, but it works. If you honey talk a man, he will do anything for you.

For women, if you want the guy to fix something, you say to him, "I'm having trouble getting . . . (fill in the blank)." Preferably not in a face-to-face situation, but while you're involved in something else. Give it a try. You may not like the answer you get—it may seem wrong to you, or it may seem like some caveman thing, but Gottman's research indicates that a woman's ability to honey talk a man is one of the master skills for relationship success.

So the two secrets are these:

1. A man's ability to say "Okay, honey."
2. A woman's ability to give lighthearted feedback and honey talk.

Those are the predictors of marital success and relationship success in general. So if you hear someone ever say, "So what I hear you saying is . . . " you know they either have been in sensitivity training or are therapy graduates.

## The Facial Expression of Divorce

I was trained by John Gottman in the early 2000s, and he showed us a few of his tricks. One of those tricks is how he can (with 85 percent accuracy) determine whether a couple will be married or divorced in the not-so-distant future by watching a five-minute segment of them talking about a neutral topic.

What he looked for was the *turning toward, turning away, and turning against* phrases I have already described, and a particular facial expression. He said this facial expression is the physical manifestation of *contempt*, and the more times he sees this the more he knows that they have relationship poison. It is a pulling back of one side of the mouth and the eye roll. You've seen it in almost every sitcom with the bright, attractive wife and the dimwitted, dumpy husband. That is *contempt*.

You may be thinking to yourself, "I've seen that every day at work." If you do that to other people, you are indicating to them, "I despise you." Like every super power, with great power comes great responsibility. Rather than focus on everyone else who has the facial expression of contempt and pointing your finger, I want you to look in the mirror.

How often do you show the facial expression of contempt?

You can't control what other people do with their faces, but you *can* control your own facial expressions.

## Love Life Success Story

One day I was interpreting some test results for the president of a company, Mike (not his real name). The assessment I was interpreting had a section for a person's judgment at work and another for a person's judgment outside of work. As I was going through the results for several people in his company, I came to one and said, "This guy is really strong at work, but it looks like he is a little distracted outside of work." Mike said, "Oh, I had to fire him. He is a great guy, fine to be around, but he kept missing work." I asked what was going on. He said, "His son was having some trouble with the law and his dad is a drunk. He kept leaving work in the middle of the day to get his son from jail or his dad from the drunk tank. I tried to make it work, but he was missing more work than he was attending. I couldn't afford to keep him on."

If you're having trouble at home, you're going to have trouble at work.

As I've watched Mike and the growth of his company from a small office to a regional powerhouse, I've been impressed that his life is *boring*. And I say that as a compliment.

Boring is good. Boring is stable. Unhappy families are each unhappy in their own way. Happy families are all alike and pretty dull—no drama. But that stability provides the launching point for adventures and success.

Mike loves his wife. He loves his kids. He makes it a practice to be home to have a family meal. His wife, an educated professional, decided to stay home to raise the kids. He talks about the way they work together to solve problems. He praises her insight and credits her observations for much of their success. Heck, they even wrote a parenting book together!

He's one of those people who has continued to call me, long after our work together had finished. He sometimes asks me for guidance. It always seems that whatever I tell him was what he was already planning—he just wanted another perspective. Mike makes excellent decisions, sometimes hard ones, but still wants someone else to chime in. I'm sure he's already talked it through with his closest advisor, his wife. I feel flattered that he's even asked me after talking to her.

## Self-Assessment

How would you rate your Love Life?

---

Awful                                                                    Happy and Content

  1        2        3        4        5        6        7        8        9        10

---

Mark this page so you can transfer your score to the summary page at the end of the book.

You can also download the full evaluation of the Big 10 from DrRogerHall.com

*Regularly review how you are doing in all 10 areas. If you monitor them, you can manage them.*

## Steps to Improve Your Love Life

1.  Monitor your conversations with your loved ones. Do you primarily turn toward, against, or away? Remind yourself that your phone, the television, or the computer are all distractions that make you turn away from your loved one. That is relationship poison.

2.  Monitor your facial expression of contempt. Look up Paul Ekman's work and see what contempt looks like.

3.  Shape your conversation for the audience. Face to face or side to side—depending on who it is.

4.  Men—learn to say (and mean it), "Okay, honey. Sure thing, babe. Yes, dear." They all work equally well.

5.  Ladies—learn to honey talk your man. It helps him regulate his mood and pull him out of flooding.

# SOCIAL LIFE

*We all need friends to tell us the truth. Successful people work very hard to find friends who run at the same speed, solve the same kinds of problems, and who share their values.*

Social life is an important and rich aspect of a happy life. There are three main aspects you should consider: First, do you have an adequate social support network? Second, ask yourself, "Who are the people I'm spending the most time with?" Third, do those people help you to improve your life, help you be happy, or do they bring you down?

The five or six people you spend most of your time with influence your thinking, for good or for bad. Supportive, positive people, some of whom share or at least understand your goals for success in your life, will help you. People who drain you of emotional resources or don't share your drive for success are making it harder for you to reach your goals.

## Friends Can Change Your Life

### Social Support

When we look at, analyze, and study social life, what we've found is that social support networks are important for recovery from illness. This includes close friends and family, for most people.

For example, in the early days of the AIDS epidemic before we had antiret-roviral drugs, if you contracted HIV, it was a death sentence. Researchers looked at what predicted the likelihood that a person who had HIV would progress to full-blown AIDS and die, and how long it would take them. What they found was that both the *quality* and the *quantity* of social sup-port was a good predictor of a person's physical outcome.

In other words, if you are ill and have no support from friends or family, then you'll tend to stay sick longer. You don't have to have a small horde of friends, but you need people you can trust—people who share your values and understand what you want to do with your life.

It's both the *quantity* and *quality* of social support that makes a difference. You might be saying to yourself, "Well, I have one really good friend and that's enough." If you've only got one really good friend and adversity strikes you (and it will at some point in your life), and you reach out to that friend on Monday night and pour out your heart, you'll feel better. Then you call on Tuesday night and cry for an hour and a half, then call on Wednesday and talk for a couple more hours.

On Thursday, your friend is going to screen your call. You need to share the wealth of your misery. You need to have a Monday friend, a Tuesday friend, a Wednesday friend, etc. They may love you, but they will get worn out.

People deal with adversity differently. Even if you're one who wants to deal with your issues yourself, sometimes you need help from others. I've had adversity in my life and thank heaven I had five buddies. I had my Monday buddy, my Tuesday buddy . . . and so on, so I could divide the pain. I had quality and quantity social support.

How many close friends you need is variable. However, if you've only got one good, high-quality, trusted friend, you might want to start reaching out more to people.

# We're primarily social creatures. We're designed to read the facial expressions of others.

Some people are really extroverted and have lots and lots of friends—but if they have a thousand friends but no good, close friends, that network is worthless.

## Evaluate the People You Spend the Most Time With

Think about the five or six people you spend the most time with in your life. At home, at work, at the gym, on weekends. These people can influence your success and your happiness. Well-known ideas about how happiness and success in your life are influenced by the people closest to you have come from Zig Ziglar and Jim Rohn, among others. If some of the people you spend most of your time with aren't helping you move toward your goals for happiness and success, it may be time to consider a change.

Highly productive, driven people often don't have many friends. So, the successful ones work really hard to find friends who are like them. For example, it's much easier for executives in a company to find other executives in that same company at that same level.

Entrepreneurs and business owners are often by themselves—they look for people who are like them and they typically can't find people with the same pressures they have. If you're a VP in a large organization, at the end of the day you don't have to make payroll on Friday—that's somebody else's job. But if you're self-employed or have a small business and have to make payroll—nobody who hasn't faced it really understands that pressure. Nobody but an entrepreneur understands mortgaging your house to pay your employees this week. So, very achievement-oriented people are often challenged to find friends, and the truly successful ones have to work hard at it.

What makes a good friend is defined differently by men and women. However, both genders count on them in the same ways. For me, if you call up a buddy to help you move and he actually shows up, he'll eventually be there to carry your casket.

## Face to Face Versus Side by Side

Men define their relationships by the activities they do with people. Women are more likely to define their relationships by who they talk with. And women are far more comfortable with eye-to-eye communication. They will look you in the eye. If you look at a man straight in the eyes for longer than a few seconds, he's going to begin wondering if you're trying to start a fight.

Men prefer to do things with other people and they define their relationships that way: this is my golfing buddy, this is my hunting buddy, this is my darts buddy, this is my football buddy. Men prefer activities where they are side to side with each other, looking at another task. As I described in the Love Life chapter, they prefer to have conversations while they're doing an activity. That way, if the conversation is going well they'll continue on with it. If one of them is uncomfortable, they always have something else there to talk about.

## Economic Parity

If you come into money, the difficulty can be that your real friends will want economic parity. Your friendship depends on you understanding that and working to make sure there is non-monetary economic parity in the relationship.

Economic parity plays out like this: if I've got a buddy and we go the movies and he forgets his wallet, I'll buy his ticket. The next time we go out, he'll say, "Hey Roger. You got my ticket last time. I got you this time."

Cool. We'll balance back and forth—that is economic parity.

**Real friendship is giving in equal amounts: money, time, and effort.**

But let's say I become famously wealthy, and now the cost of a trip to the Bahamas is proportionately what it used to cost me to go to the movies. I say to my buddy, "Hey, Bill, do you want to come to the Bahamas with me?" What happens? He'll say he can't afford it and can't repay me. I say, "It's okay, I've got it," because it's like a movie ticket for me.

The next time he wants to go out with me, he calls me up and says, "Hey, Roger, do you want to go to the movies? I'm buying." Does he feel like he has economic parity with me? No. Most likely he's going to feel like a mooch. So the dynamic of the relationship changes. If he is brave, eventually my friend is going to say, "Roger, we can't run together anymore because I can't keep up." Either he will fade away or he'll become a suck-up—the guy who says ridiculous things like, "Roger, you are so smart. You are so wonderful." He ceases to be a friend and instead becomes part of my entourage.

You need friends who will fight for authenticity in the relationship. Each of you provides non-monetary economic parity. We each give to the relationship things of value that aren't related to money. Things like trust, laughter, keeping things private, and so on. They have to know that your friendship is more than just about the give and take of money.

## Everybody Wants to Beat Up on Tiger

A few years before this writing, golf professional Tiger Woods was in the news quite a bit, and it wasn't good press.

What was Tiger Woods' biggest problem? He didn't have anybody who would kick him in the butt. There was nobody from his life (possibly since his father died), who would say "Tiger, you are out of line and if you keep this up, I'm going to kick your butt."

Tiger had achieved success and it appears that it separated him from any friends he had. He didn't appear to be able to find new ones who understood where he was at. We all need friends who will point out when we're off the tracks. People who aren't intimidated by the big house and fancy car or who aren't out to get something from you. If you don't cultivate those honest friends, you will find yourself surrounded by kiss-ups and toadies.

If you don't have that economic parity with your friends and you start running with people who you feel you can "own" or who feel like they owe you something, you stop being friends. It's important that you find people with whom you have economic parity—authentic friends who see past your success and will tell you the difficult truth. You need somebody who will hold you accountable. If you don't have that person in your life, you can run into all kinds of trouble.

### How Do You Find More Friends?

Good relationships take *years* to develop. If you build a relationship on an intense experience, it's building a house on a card table—I call it the psychology of extreme experiences. You're out of your element and it's stressful and it's intoxicating. That's why, in the movie *Mission Impossible 2*, Tom Cruise ends up in bed with the beautiful woman after the car chase, because they've had this extreme experience. That experience makes them believe they're closer than they really are, but there's no foundation there—no trust, no common ground beyond that extreme experience (and it *is* the movies).

# Friendships are built on nickel-and-dime conversations and shared experiences that develop trust.

The law of reciprocity is another case of extremes with no stable foundation. It's even, but it's extreme. The law of reciprocity is that if I give you something of value, you will return something of value to me. So, if I give you an intimate self-disclosure (compared to nickel-and-dime conversations, this would be a high-dollar disclosure) and tell you some deep-dark secret of my life, what do you feel compelled to do? Double down. You give *me* a heartfelt secret you've never told anyone else—a valuable self-disclosure. Then we feel we're bonded, we're connected. No, you're not! You've just exchanged too much information too soon. And that's the house of cards that lots of toxic relationships get built on.

Psychotherapy or executive coaching is built on an uneven relationship. You tell me your intimate self-disclosures and I promise not to tell anyone. And you don't get any of mine because I promise not to tell anybody. That works because it's a constrained, professional relationship. It doesn't work if you're giving that self-disclosure on a talk show. Then everybody knows!

If you want to build a strong relationship, you have to start slow. It can be intoxicating if somebody reveals a deep dark secret to you. And you feel really, really connected to them. That's a sham! That's a lie. That's like infatuation and its relationship to love. It's a passing fancy and it's going to go away. If you want to have really great relationships, you have to build them for years. And if you've only got one good friend and you're 60 years old, you better spend your 60s building some more. Because you're not going to know if you can trust them until you're about 70.

You find friends based on your values. Do they have the same set of values as you do? Those values are the moral decisions you make. And I don't mean just religious decisions, I mean how do you treat one another? That's how you choose. It's like interviewing an employee. You may go through lots of interviews before you find the right ones. Recreational and spiritual life activities are good places to find people with shared values.

## Social Life Success Story

A friend and colleague of mine is a great example of a person being intentional about his social network. Jim (not his real name) and I worked together for about five years. Throughout that time, he was intentional that his business was going to be a team. He had the value of friends working together and playing together. He was and is an avid road bicyclist. Many of the people on his team rode with him.

At one point, one of our mutual friends was going through a rough time in his work life. Eric (not his real name) was the leader of his organization. He was a powerful, decisive leader with a heart of gold, but he had a physical presence that could easily intimidate people who wanted a cushy job. (If you have ever read any of Lee Child's books about the character Jack Reacher, this guy could have played the part in the movies and been more believable than Tom Cruise.) Isolated, alone, and frequently misunderstood, the board of directors decided Eric needed to go. It was at this point that Jim and I got the chance to support him. In a car with Eric sitting in the back seat, his knees folded up around the shoulders of his 6' 7" frame, we discussed ways we could shift some new work to our friend so he could continue to support his family. It wasn't "charity," it was helping a buddy in the middle of a hard time. My road-biking friend Jim invited Eric to start riding with him.

In a very short time, Eric was leading the pack on the road and leading the pack in our business. With a new team around him, his strengths could be showcased. It wasn't long before we were adopting his ideas and practices. He became a central part of our business.

Eric had a team at his old job, and as Jim often says, it was the team he as the leader deserved . . . i.e., before he woke up. Once he discovered what a team with the right fit was like—with shared values, inspired drive, and purpose—the result was deeply fulfilling, sustainable, and produced great fruit in his life and the lives of others.

Again, this wasn't charity. Jim and I had hundreds of nickel-and-dime interactions with Eric over the years, before bringing him in to our company. In the end, we all gained more from him than we ever gave to him. Had he not developed the relationships, he would have been alone, out on the end of a long string, wondering what would happen next. Once he found the tribe who shared his values and purpose, he was able to thrive and helped to change the lives of thousands. I'm still grateful for his influence today.

## Self-Assessment

How would you rate your Social Life?

---

Lonely and Isolated                                      Strong and Enough

| 1 | 2 | 3 | 4 | 5 | 6 | 7 | 8 | 9 | 10 |

---

Mark this page so you can transfer your score to the summary page at the end of the book.

You can also download the full evaluation of the Big 10 from DrRogerHall.com

*Regularly review how you are doing in all 10 areas. If you monitor them, you can manage them.*

## Steps to Improve Your Social Life

1. Assess the quality of your friends. Do you have enough? Are they people who build you up or make you feel lousy?

2. Start now. It takes about a decade to develop a true friend.

3. Start slow. Again—it takes about a decade to develop a true friend. Beware of the psychology of extreme experiences. Start with nickel-and-dime conversations.

4. Fish in the right ponds. Spend time on social gatherings of people who are likely to share your values (religious, economic, political, and so on).

5. One great way to learn about a person is to share a meal.

## WORK LIFE

*Humans are built to work. We're designed to love our work. Having work with purpose and accomplishment is important for happiness in your life.*

### Built to Work

Human beings crave meaningful work. If you are counting down your days to retirement, please read this section completely and consider placing it near the top of your list of things to work on. Having meaningful work is one of the foundations of a successful life.

Some people tell me, "I can't wait until I retire. Work is terrible."

They say, "I'm going to golf 36 holes and lay around and read the paper."

But those people will likely be dead within five years, if they don't find something else to do. You know why? We are built to work. We are most happy when we are solving problems in our domain of expertise. Don't mistake me—what we don't like is *toil.*

# We are built to work.

For a period of my life, I lived near King's Island, the amusement park. When we moved there, my kids yelped, "You mean we can get a season pass and go to King's Island every day?"

I said, "Yes." We bought a season pass and every Sunday, we went to King's Island for a couple hours, all summer long. The next summer we bought a season pass and we went to King's Island twice. The next summer, I said, "You guys want a King's Island pass?" And they said, "No, not really. It's kind of boring."

King's Island is a great example of recreation. We think recreation is the end goal of life, but it's not. We can find some pleasure and fun in recreation, but where we find the most happiness is in our work.

## Where we find the most happiness is in our work.

Happiness and pleasure are two different things. Pleasure, entertainment, distraction, and fun are all good things. But they are transitory—they fade quickly. Happiness lasts longer. Researchers in this area often make it synonymous to "life satisfaction." It is a more stable, positive mood.

## Your Work Needs to Have Meaning

### "FOBbits" and Rangers

FOB is the abbreviation for a *forwarding operating base* in wartime. People who lived in the forward operation base were sometimes derisively called "fobbits." Typically, unit cohesion was bad in the FOBs because people who were dressed for war, ready for battle, and carrying rifles were standing around doing nothing. They were all dressed up with no place to go.

Rangers, on the other hand, were outside the wire, busting down doors, clearing houses, and killing insurgents. They had very dangerous work (with its own negative consequences), but unit cohesion was high because they had a *purpose* and they needed their teammates to safely do their job.

Every day, they had something to do that really mattered. And it really mattered that they got along with the people next to them or they'd be dead.

Back on the FOB, they're doing accounting and polishing trucks, some of them just trying to keep busy. They didn't do well. So, having work that has purpose and accomplishment is very important for morale, which leads to your happiness in life.

## Getting in the Zone: Flow

I do fun work, where nearly every day I get to solve complex problems in my domain of expertise. That is the formula for lasting happiness.

Back in the 1980s, a Hungarian researcher, Mihaly Csikszentmihalyi, got interested in the psychology of the optimal experience. Yes, that is his name. It is pronounced "Me-high Check-sent-me-high-ee" (emphasis on the first syllable)—no, I'm not making this up. When I first butchered the pronunciation of his name in public a helpful Hungarian woman wrote out the correct pronunciation that I still have tucked in his book *Flow: The Psychology of the Optimal Experience*. His friends call him Mike—which is helpful for those linguistically challenged people who have trouble ordering at a Mexican restaurant (like me). Heaven help us at a Hungarian restaurant.

At the time, researchers were looking really hard at pathology, and the Positive Psychology movement hadn't taken off. Csikszentmihalyi was an early proponent of the best of human experience and was considered one of the founders, along with Martin Seligman, of the Positive Psychology movement. Csikszentmihalyi wanted to know what was happening to people when they felt good or happy.

He gave his participants beepers to carry around (it was the '80s). At random times, he would page them and ask them to write down what they were doing and how they felt. What he found was that they seemed to be immersed in solving a problem when they reported being happy. He found two basic qualities of this state: 1. Feeling one with the work. 2. Losing a sense of time.

He found it happened for surgeons in the middle of surgery (though they weren't as likely to write down how they felt at that exact moment), chess masters in the midst of the game, and other people when they were in the middle of their work. He coined the term for this state: *flow*.

The way I define flow is this: when you are solving a challenging problem in your domain of expertise, you are in flow.

When I am giving a speech, solving a people problem, or working on a thinking problem, I am in flow. I lose the sense of time and feel joined with my work. These are my domains of expertise.

I never feel flow when I am solving plumbing problems. These are challenging problems and NOT in my domain of expertise. In those times, I feel anxiety. I sure hope plumbers feel flow when they are solving plumbing problems.

What Csikszentmihalyi found was that people didn't experience flow when they were at a ball game, at the movies, or recreating. They were having fun, but fun isn't the same as flow. In sports, they call it "the zone." You remember when Michael Jordan was shooting these crazy three pointers and he wasn't missing? I remember after he drained one of those shots, he made a sort of embarrassed smile, raised his hands in that "I don't understand how this is happening" sign, and then ran down the court to grab the next rebound. He was in flow. The zone.

You may have had the experience of getting into the zone when you worked on certain kinds of problems—maybe it was working on your car or working on your house. You were so focused that suddenly you looked up and realized, "Oh my gosh. I've been doing this for three hours."

# The experience of flow is where most people find the greatest amount of happiness.

Being able to lose yourself in the task you are doing contributes to a sense of accomplishment and life satisfaction—happiness. People report a greater sense of happiness when they can daily slip into the flow than if they go to King's Island every day. And where is getting into the flow most likely to happen? At work—if you are working at the right job for you.

If you are in a workplace where you don't experience flow, where you are not able to concentrate on a task that you can easily lose yourself in solving, then you will not be happy. There are thousands and thousands of people who do not experience flow at their work. Perhaps this is why workplace engagement, as measured by the Gallup organization, is abysmally low. (You can look it up yourself, but the results have been pretty much the same for years—about 20 percent of the people are engaged or actively engaged in work, about 60 percent are neither engaged nor disengaged at work, and about 20 percent are either disengaged or *actively* disengaged at work. It's important to emphasize that a not insignificant percentage of workers are *actively* disengaged at work. They are the people who are trying to mess things up. Throwing wrenches in the gears. Jamming the printer to slow work down.)

There are thousands of people in soul-crushing jobs where their employer has no interest in what revs their engines. This is too bad—and a sucky way to live your life. If you don't experience flow every day or nearly every day at work, there are plenty of other jobs; find another one if you want to be happy.

I'm not saying work that has flow for you is necessarily easy. It likely is not. Every great job has its bad days. And not every day has a bundle of flow. I have to do my taxes, fight with technology, and pay bills just like everyone else. Those are not flow days for me, but that work still needs to be done. You'll have those days too.

## Happiness at Work

### Be an Expert

Work is where we get our pleasure and our happiness. The trick is finding the kind of work that creates flow for you—that lets you slip into the zone.

If I'm solving plumbing problems, that's a day of hell for me because I'm not really good at solving plumbing problems. But a plumber, or someone who is good at plumbing, will have a good day because they got to solve problems in their domain of expertise. People who are bookkeepers and accountants, they love diving into numbers. They can't wait to do that because it's their domain of expertise.

Happiness is more correlated with productive work (being in that state of flow) than almost any other thing. You can improve your mood by physical exercise and by solving a problem in your domain of expertise. You may say "Well, I don't really do that at work, but I have this hobby. I like woodworking. I like fixing things." Whatever it is, that's your domain of expertise. Make sure you are an expert at something you truly enjoy— some mental or physical activity that engages your mind. That's where happy, productive work comes from. And happy, productive work is a major factor in a happy, productive life.

## Don't Ever Retire

We all need to work. I regularly recommend to people, "Don't ever retire." You can stop working for money, but then you need to start working for something else.

There was a couple who made millions in real estate and they didn't need to work anymore, but they loved people. They didn't really want a lot of heavy responsibility, so they both got jobs as Wal-Mart greeters—and they absolutely love it. They get to meet people all day and kibitz a little with no responsibility.

When it is time for you to retire from your current job, come up with a plan for what you want to do next. If it's volunteering for an activity that you love, if it's investing your time to develop your grandchildren, come up with that plan ahead of time. Otherwise you will probably die too young.

## Who Invited This Guy?

My father was a university professor from 1965 until he retired in 1995. At my father's retirement party, a man he knew came up to him and said, "George, today is the worst day of your life. When you walk out that door, nobody will ask your opinion and all of your work will be forgotten. You're making a mistake."

I thought, "Who invited this guy?"

I began to get a little bit worried about my dad. He is well known for having an easygoing, happy disposition. I wondered if retirement would turn him into a bitter man.

Dad's university retirement agreement required that he remain off-campus for 30 days, as the university didn't want faculty working continuously and double dipping. So he left campus for 30 days.

On day 31, he drove back to campus at 7:30 a.m., climbed four flights of stairs to his office, put on a pot of coffee, and went back to work. He worked every day for the next 10 years without pay.

Fortunately, he was receiving his retirement pay and pension, so lack of money was not an issue. He said it was the best 10 years of his career. You know why? He said it was because he didn't have to do any of the stuff that he didn't want to do and he got to focus on doing all the stuff he liked to do.

## Doing work you enjoy will lead you to a productive life, whether or not you're getting paid for it.

My dad went back to work not for the sake of money but for the sake of spending his life doing something that was meaningful for him. People thought he was nuts for working without pay. He didn't have a need for money, but he did have the need to do productive work and he recognized it. He continued to be the happy, easygoing person we all know.

## Work Life Success Story

One of the men who later became a mentor in my life was a work colleague. One day, he came to me and asked me a question: "Roger, I've got two guys who have applied to become the janitor. One guy really needs the job, but I'm not too sure how well he could do the job. The other guy doesn't need the job, but I know he would do a better job. Who do you think I should hire?"

I told him that I thought he should hire the guy who would do a better job. So my mentor did.

I didn't interact much with the new guy, Rick (not his real name), outside of small talk. I remember walking past a closet where he was putting up shelves. I stuck my head inside to say hello and what I saw made me a little nervous about the quality of my advice. There he was, with a hammer and a nail and about 50 nail holes all over the walls. Holes like tiny machine gun fire. No measuring tape, no bubble level. Just holes all over the drywall.

> "Uh, whatcha doing?"
> "I'm looking for the studs."
> "Oh, ok."

About three hours later, I walked past the closet, fearing a disaster. What I saw made my jaw drop. All the solid wood shelving had been installed, plumb and true. Rick had trimmed out all the pieces, put on a coat of stain, and was finishing painting the walls. Not a single hole to be found. In fact, it looked perfect.

"Where are all the holes?"

"I patched them."

Never before had I seen a more productive worker. Over the months and years we worked together, I learned more and more about this unlikely man. While he was working full time as a janitor for us, he was also working in a video store (this was the era of videocassettes). You may have stereotypes about guys who work as janitors and moonlight in video stores. I had them too. The more I learned about him, the more I learned that I had massively underestimated him.

Rick was a retired career Air Force firefighter, station chief, and an Airman's Medal recipient who had pulled a pilot out of a burning airplane. He had a full military retirement check coming in each month that he was saving. He wasn't working for money. He took the janitor job because he wanted to keep busy. He took the video store job because he wanted to learn that business.

In a relatively short period of time, Rick took his own video collection and made that the initial stock for his own video store. A few years later, he sold that profitable store and went on to try his hand at a new business. After a few years, he sold that next business and moved to another state where he promptly got a job as a cashier at a gas station (any guesses at how that turned out?). Now he runs the regional truck stop, created with its own petting zoo, all the while owning and running a separate manufacturing company.

Why? Because Rick *loves* to work. As he and I became friends, I learned that whatever he put his hand to, he would inevitably turn it into success. Has he experienced adversity? Of course he has. Is he one of the happier people I know? Absolutely! Happily married, enjoying his many enthusiasms, helping people every day in his work, and loving life. He is one of the most successful people I know.

Be careful how you evaluate people. Sometimes the most successful ones look nothing like the traditional image of success, but in every case of really successful people, they love their work.

## Self-Assessment

How would you rate your Work Life?

Soul Crushing                                        Life Affirming and Meaningful

| 1 | 2 | 3 | 4 | 5 | 6 | 7 | 8 | 9 | 10 |

Mark this page so you can transfer your score to the summary page at the end of the book.

You can also download the full evaluation of the Big 10 from DrRogerHall.com

*Regularly review how you are doing in all 10 areas. If you monitor them, you can manage them.*

## Steps to Improve Your Work Life

1. Take another look at the self-rating number you just circled above. If you rated your work as soul crushing, it's time to look for new work. However, don't quit your day job until you know what you love. There are plenty of online resources to help you discover the types of jobs you might love. Look into the work of John Holland. He was a career researcher who developed a robust career interest model. Search his work, find an online assessment, and discover if you are in the right kind work.

2. Look at when you experience flow. That will give you a clue to what lights your jets.

3. People join companies for the work and leave because of a bad boss. Look hard at your situation and ask yourself, "Do I hate the work or do I have a bad boss?" If it is a bad boss, look for similar work with different people.

4. If you feel compelled to stay in a job for some other reasons (security, benefits, etc.), then make sure your outside of work time is filled with activities that help you achieve flow.

5. Never retire!

# MONEY LIFE

*Money can't buy you happiness, but it sure can help you to avoid a lot of misery. And if you have more than you can handle, it can **create** misery unless you get help to learn how.*

## Too Much Money Problems

Money can't buy you happiness (you've heard this before). But money sure can help you avoid misery. How much? That's subjective, but we can talk about some practical limits that make sense to everyone.

Here's a little of what we know from research on money and happiness:

Imagine a number line with income numbers from negative numbers to zero and then extending into billions of dollars. When people have less than a certain amount of money (near, at, or below zero), they're miserable. Yes, you can be happy in those times, but the results of studies confirm that the lack of money will make you miserable.

Because, let's face it, life is hard if you have no money or are deep in debt. Yes, you can have happiness in poverty. But I'm not going to tell people, "Oh you don't need money." Obviously you need money to buy food. If you don't have food, life is miserable. If you are sleeping under a bridge, life is miserable.

Then there is a range on the income number line where people feel they have enough money. I don't define the top or the bottom end of this range, but we find that people tend to be very happy in this segment where they feel they have enough money. Some researchers have "defined" that amount, but it's a relative number—if you are a single income earner with four kids in the Bay Area, then that amount of money will buy you a lot less than a single person with no dependents living in Oklahoma.

When we look at self-reports of happiness, we find that happiness is also pretty low until you get to that "enough money" level. Once people get that amount of money, they'll report happiness. But once they reach this "enough money" segment of the number line of income, most people need four times as much money to get one additional increment of happiness.

This range is pretty long on the income number line, but then there is another cutoff point and beyond that, life satisfaction seems to go down again. When people start to move beyond the "enough money" amount, that's where we find people who have what I refer to as "too much money" problems. This "too much money" segment of the number line is different for everyone. Warren Buffett has figured out how to be happy with billions. Others are destroyed by too much money, even a million dollars.

You may be saying to yourself right now, "I'd like to try that out." I've worked with some very high net worth individuals and they have "too much money" problems. It's real and many wish they didn't have that much money. These people often don't know who their friends are (remember Tiger Woods?). They usually have people around them who are sponging off them because of the access to money. But they may not know who loves them for themselves. Imagine that, if you can.

You may be thinking, "I could live with that." Maybe . . . just maybe you could, but many wealthy people report being happier *before* they had all their money.

Handling a lot of money successfully takes knowledge—an understanding of what's important. Many people require education to learn how to effectively handle a lot of money, and that can be a complicating factor.

This is even more important if your income has increased dramatically in recent years. Although you may not be a lottery gambler, it's interesting to note the statistics on lottery winners. After receiving half of their winnings, lottery winners only saved 16 cents of every dollar won.[5] One statistic, quoted by financial advisor Ric Edelman, stated that one third of lottery winners spend all of their winnings within five years of the award.[6] A sudden, publicized increase in their personal worth can have devastating consequences for their personal lives and can make them a target for opportunistic people.

Henry Ford, who was very wealthy, said he was never happier than before he made his money. In hindsight, that money created a lot of problems for him.

When John Paul Getty owned Standard Oil, people would come to his house and make long-distance phone calls. Back then, a long-distance call was very expensive. His house guests likely made the rationalization that "compared to all the money he has, he won't even notice that I made this three-hour call to Afghanistan." In relative terms, that money was a rounding error in his life, but it was *his* money they were spending—they took advantage of him and felt justified because of his wealth. What did he do? He installed pay phones in every guest room. It made him look like a miserly cheapskate—but they were spending *his* money without his permission. I feel bad for all the wealthy people I know who have others take advantage of their wealth.

## The Cost of One Fine Thing

More money can create new problems you never considered before. Suppose you want a mansion. Then you need to figure out how you're going to clean the place. "Well, I'll just hire a housekeeper." Then you'll likely have personnel problems. They'll want benefits and then you will have to deal with employees who don't show up on time, employees who quit unexpectedly, or employees whose kids need orthodontics. So, do you really want the big house and all the problems that come with it?

## A Free Mule

Here's a great parable about the cost of a free mule that I learned from Don Aslett's book *For Packrats Only: How to Clean Up, Clear Out, and Dejunk Your Life Forever:*

A man was given a free mule. He thought it would be great on his little property, so he took the free mule. Then he realized he had to fence the whole property with an electrified fence. Then he needed to bring in hay. Then he had to get all the equipment to water and feed and shelter the mule. It eventually cost him about $10,000 for that free mule.

You need to determine the maintenance cost of the life you want. A friend of mine said, "Money doesn't change you, it only magnifies what's already there."

## Lack of Money Problems

A few words on "lack of money" problems. The successful people I know have figured out a way through their lack of money problems. With rare exception, these people have had at least one, and for many, several times when they've been broke. I've found in my study of really successful people that most were *not* born with a silver spoon in their mouths. You want to know how trust fund babies typically live? They are 35 years old, playing Xbox in the basement of a house their parents bought them, smoking really good weed. That is as good as it is going to get for them, and in my mind, this is not success.

Being out of money is a valuable lesson that all successful people have learned from. The thing that successful people know is this: Being poor is fundamentally different than being out of money or broke. Being poor requires an attitude of "Who will take care of me?"

**Being broke is simply the fact of being out of money.**

Successful people who are out of money figure out how to make money again, pay off their debt, and get ahead. Unsuccessful people give up. They ask, "Why won't someone take care of me?"

I've been broke. I've accidently bounced checks. I've paid overdraft fees because I would have bounced checks otherwise. I've been denied credit cards because my credit rating was too low. I've been so in debt I didn't exactly know how I'd get out (and it took me years to fix), but I was never poor—because I never stopped trying to figure out how to fix the problem.

Lying awake at night worried about how you are going to pay your bills is a pretty good way to feel miserable, but it is a problem that can be solved. I have a successful friend who said, "If it is a problem you can solve with money, it isn't that big of a problem." That is an attitude difference that characterizes successful people.

You might want to know that the successful people I know rarely have the desire to make a ton of money. They have a desire to make a cool product, serve people with their expertise, or come up with a better system to solve a problem. The abundance of money is a side effect of their life success, not their end goal.

# For the successful people I know, the money is a side effect of their life success.

If you have lack of money problems now, you are not alone. As I said, almost all of the successful people I've worked with have been in the same spot. If you believe you can never be a success because you don't have much money or are in debt, then the first thing you need to change is your mindset, not your bank account.

## Improving Your Money Life

### Handling Money Is a Skill

Having worked with many high net worth people, I view money a lot like electricity.

I feel safe and comfortable with a standard household outlet—a 110-volt outlet. Why? I've been trained on how to use that. I've used it a lot in my life. The plug behind my dryer—the 220—I'm a little bit afraid of that one. I haven't spent as much time using that. If you put me on a utility pole, what will happen to me? I may very well end up dead because it's *too much power.* How do electrical workers do their work without dying? They've been trained!

It's the same with money. The amount of money you deal with every day, you're safe with. If you get a little extra money and you don't have much training, that should scare you a little. But if you get *lots* of money right away with no training, you'll very likely get burned if you don't get some help from a professional.

An electrical lineman with adequate training is fine on the transformer pole because he/she knows how to use the power. Part of good use of money is like any use of power—it requires training so it doesn't destroy your life.

### Money Resources

If you think your money life could be improved with more knowledge about how to handle it, bring someone into your life that is smarter than you about money to teach you. You can hire someone to help or educate yourself through books or training.

You can hire a money advisor such as a financial planner. There are online experts, book series, and published authors such as Dave Ramsey, David Bach, Suze Orman, Ric Edelman, Nick Murray, the Wealthy Barber, Cory Fawcett's *The Doctors Guide* series, and TED Talks.

## Little money or lots of money, you need to choose for yourself the lifestyle you want.

Figure out the life you want and then use money to fuel that life.

### Money Life Success Story

My best friend's father-in-law is a great example of Thomas Stanley's and William Danko's *The Millionaire Next Door: The Surprising Secrets of America's Wealthy (Taylor Trade Publishing, 2010)*. When we watch the lifestyles of celebrities on TV, we begin to think that rich people live large, drink Dom Perignon, and eat caviar. When we listen to the news, they love to talk about "corporate fat cats," like anyone who owns a business takes a limo to his or her yacht for a weekend in Nassau. The popular cultural image is that the purpose of money is to buy fancy things and live in luxury.

Stanley's and Danko's book blows the doors off that image. The prototypical car of the millionaire next door is an F-150. The typical millionaire still clips coupons and looks for deals (honest, they do). For many of them, the purpose of money is freedom. The freedom to be left alone, the freedom from worry, the freedom to give their money to things they care about.

Carl (not his real name), my friend's father-in-law, is a great example of that millionaire next door model. He grew up in an enormous family by today's standards, though at the time it would have been a slightly larger than average Catholic family. He went to school with people who looked different than he did and took a job as a picker while he was a teenager. When he was picking walnuts, his hands turned so black that his teachers wouldn't let him hold the books because his fingers would stain the pages.

Eventually, his father turned him onto the scrap metal business (as if that would clean up his hands). He went to the "finest" local community college and lasted all of one semester before he dropped out to work the scrapping business.

The husband of his high school sweetheart, when Carl retired he was one of the scrap metal leaders in his area. Not exactly glamorous work, but he was able to earn a good living. So what does he do with his wealth? Well, he loves to go to Chick-Fil-A, get his free cup of senior coffee and his dollar meal. He likes to drive his decade-old SUV. He likes to travel to visit with his kids and grandkids. And he loves to give his money to support missionaries—perhaps dozens of them (he's probably intentionally unclear about his giving, because it isn't his way to brag). Carl and his wife collected household donations for missionaries in Papua New Guinea and packed them in 40-foot shipping containers—three times a year, for fifteen years. For him, the purpose of money is not a fancy life, it is the opportunity to give.

When my eldest son moved to Carl's area three weeks before Christmas, Carl and his wife invited my son to spend Christmas day with them. They invited a young stranger into their home to share Christmas so he wouldn't have to be alone. Using wealth to help others have better lives—that seems like success to me.

Almost all of the people I work with who are very successful look a lot like the millionaires next door. Honest, down-to-earth men and women who use their money for freedom to pursue their values.

## Self-Assessment

How would you rate your Money Life?

---

Money Problems (too much or too little)                    Disciplined

1        2        3        4        5        6        7        8        9        10

---

Mark this page so you can transfer your score to the summary page at the end of the book.

You can also download the full evaluation of the Big 10 from DrRogerHall.com

*Regularly review how you are doing in all 10 areas. If you monitor them, you can manage them.*

## Steps to Improve Your Money Life

1. Find someone to train you on the proper use of money. Read some of the books mentioned above. Find a millionaire next door and ask for advice, not a handout. I find that wealthy people get hit up for money way more often than for advice.

2. Determine the purpose of money for you. Is it status? Toys? Freedom? Peace of mind? Why you pursue money is often the reason it escapes you. Learn from wealthy people why they have pursued money.

3. Create value, love your work, and very often the money will be a side effect of your purposeful work.

4. If you have lack of money problems, first work on your attitude. Is your lack of money a math problem or an attitude problem? If you think it is someone else's job to take care of you, then you are likely to continue being out of money.

# SLEEP AND REST LIFE

*Your brain repairs itself while you're asleep. If you aren't sleeping well, you'll see a host of physical and emotional problems develop. Make a new habit to go to bed earlier.*

Before you can function optimally in your life, you need to take care of yourself. Getting enough rest and sleep is the first step toward maintaining your health. I'd argue that it is *the* cornerstone habit. Without first addressing your sleep problems, you may not be able to address any of the other areas in your life.

Sleep is important—maybe this is obvious, but maybe not as much as it needs to be. A great book called *The Promise of Sleep* by William Dement, a Stanford professor, describes sleep disorders and sleep problems. He argues that one of the primary reasons we have so many health problems in the United States is because we have bad sleep patterns. Many Mediterranean countries have siestas or naps to make up for less sleep at night; other countries like France have higher than average amounts of sleep.

Dement's book was published nearly 20 years ago, and the information in it is still current. Many advances have been made in scientific understanding of the role of sleep for your health and cognitive abilities, but the message hasn't changed: sleep deprivation can damage your health and diminish all of your faculties. In the United States, we would be wise to place greater emphasis on getting adequate amounts of regular sleep.

While recent studies have placed the U.S. nightly sleep average at just over seven hours (when you include the weekends—less than seven on weeknights), several countries average considerably higher, including the Netherlands, France, New Zealand, Australia, and Belgium, at over eight hours for each of these countries.

## After about age eight, most people are sleep deprived.

### Sleeping Like an Eight-Year-Old

Who in your home is getting enough sleep? Your dog and/or cat. Okay, outside of the animals, probably the youngest. After about age eight, most people are sleep deprived. There's an easy way to know if you are: If you can fall asleep in less than 20 minutes, you are probably sleep deprived.

(What if it takes a lot *longer* than 20 minutes to fall asleep? Is it because you have thoughts, worries, or the day's irritations racing around in your head? I'll talk about that next.)

Chances are, the only person in your house who's not sleep deprived is eight years old. The struggle to get your child to sleep usually takes around 20 minutes. That's how long it *should* take you to lapse from consciousness into unconsciousness.

Why are so many people sleep deprived? My theory is it started with the widespread availability of electricity. Back in the 1800s when they had oil lamps, once it got dark, what could you do? Either have sex or fall asleep. That's pretty much it (which is why they all had 14 kids). Those were the only things you could do.

Back then, people would very often wake up in the middle of the night and be awake for a couple of hours. They would talk to the people they were in bed with for an hour or two, then fall back to sleep. This was a common sleep cycle.

Now, because of electricity and all the activities you can do into the night, you may stay up very late. You may watch television—the news, the Tonight Show (or whatever), even if it's not that entertaining —or be on your computer or phone: videos, on-demand movies, texting your friends, Twitter, Facebook, Instagram, Pinterest, or Reddit. You may fall asleep on the couch and then you have to wake up again and walk into the bedroom.

All of that keeps you awake longer and creates *sleep debt.*

## Sleep Debt

What are the consequences of sleep debt? High blood pressure, heart disease, obesity, stroke—to name a few. This was reported in Dement's book in 2000, and it's still true today. All of these are big problems.

You are far less able to concentrate when you are sleepy. You can't make good decisions when your brain is fatigued.

When is the most dangerous time to be on the road—when most crashes happen? You may think it is two in the morning on Friday or Saturday night, after people leave the bars and they are drunk, right? Actually, it's rush hour on any workday and the few days following the "spring forward" daylight savings time change. Studies have shown that crashes happen on those days because people's sleep cycles have been disrupted and they lost an hour of sleep during the transition.

### Sleep Debt Is Dangerous

Driving drowsy is a much greater problem, in reality, than driving drunk. Both are preventable but happen far too often. Even if you never drink, I guarantee you, *everyone* has driven while they were sleepy—and probably even completely asleep.

If you have ever driven and had a "head snap," you've already been asleep when your chin dips down to your chest and your head snaps back. Typically, this is within five seconds after you've lapsed into unconsciousness. At 55 miles an hour, within much less than five seconds you can go left of center into oncoming traffic.

Humans will lapse into unconsciousness and are not aware of it for about five seconds. Wire people up in a lab and look at the wave pattern in their EEGs and you will recognize that they have fallen asleep. People don't even recognize that they have fallen asleep until after five seconds of being asleep. What wakes you up is the head snap.

If you read any of the details about the Exxon Valdez incident, you know the captain was drunk. He was also off duty. Yes, he was drunk, but he wasn't driving the ship.

The person driving the ship was a third mate who had had six hours of sleep in the previous 48 hours. He nodded off, missed a marker buoy, and crashed the boat into Alaska. It's the biggest state in the Union—you'd think he would have seen it.

The worst maritime oil disaster in the United States history was a result of lack of sleep, not alcohol.

## Recovering Sleep Debt

Recovering sleep debt is vitally important because if you have health problems, improving your sleep can help your body heal itself.

You may think you are good with six hours. Yes, there are ranges—some people need less and some need more. But, your mom was right—the average adult needs eight.

If you are getting significantly less than eight hours, you probably have sleep debt. How do you know that's the case? You sleep more on the weekends. You sleep in.

Sleeping in is a way to recover your sleep debt.

Many people recover their sleep debt when they are sick because they sleep all day for a couple of days and then say, "Man, I must have been really sick. I slept for a long time." That's just part of it. The other part is your body using that time to recover its sleep debt. If you don't recover your sleep debt within two weeks, there are physical consequences—aging, ill health, increased levels of cholesterol, the whole thing. So it is important that you get good sleep and enough of it.

## What's Keeping You From Falling Asleep

There are probably only two times in your day when no one is influencing your life—when it's quiet with no distractions.

One is in the shower, which is why you have all your best ideas in the shower. I am assuming most of you can take a shower and clean your body without thinking about it. You don't have to think about what you're doing, and your mind can empty.

There's one other time you don't have any distractions: when you lay your head on the pillow. That time between when your head hits the pillow and when you are lapsing into unconsciousness is when a flood of worries comes into your head. Five or 10 minutes is plenty of time for this to happen.

But here's how it works. You lie down and the thought comes into your head—and there's nothing to distract you from the troubling thought. I call it the worry loop.

Here's what happens when the worries come: You think, "I've got to remember to do that tomorrow. Don't forget that." Pretty soon you're wide awake, panicked that you will forget everything.

Many people play the radio or put the sleep timer on their TV, so they are distracted as they are lapsing into unconsciousness—so the troubling thoughts don't come.

Have you ever had one of those panic moments as you were falling asleep—did I set the alarm, did I set the alarm? Then you set four alarms just in case (maybe that's just me).

This time of undistracted quiet time also happens between three and four in the morning, when you wake and can't fall back asleep. The reason for that is when you fall asleep, it's not that you lapse into unconsciousness and stay unconscious—when you fall asleep, you pass through five distinct phases of sleep that cycle through the night.

## All You Have to Do Is Dream

The most important sleep phase is REM sleep—rapid eye movement sleep—which is when you are dreaming.

You may think you don't dream anymore, but you probably have about 50 dreams a night. A dream you remember may have seemed long, but they are compressed in time. It may have seemed like it took an hour when it was actually 30 seconds because your brain is compressing it.

You don't remember your dreams unless you wake in the middle of them. So when you wake up in the morning, if you wake in the middle of a dream, you'll forget it by the time you've been to the bathroom. Unless you rehearse the dream—tell somebody about it, write it down, think about it—you will forget the dream forever. So what's the purpose of dreams?

We don't really know, but one of the theories on dreams is this: Dreams essentially clear out the memories of the previous day, the unfinished loops of the previous day, and weave them together in a story. So if you have ever had a weird dream and it seems to have pieces of stuff that you've been thinking about recently, it's because these stray fragments of memory were woven together into a story. The combined details of your recent experiences can be startlingly odd. Your brain integrates fragmentary pieces of memory to kind of clear the decks and get rid of them. REM sleep unclutters memory fragments stored in your brain and allows you to think more clearly when you are awake.

Your body needs REM sleep. If you are deprived of REM sleep during one night, you will have more of it the next night.

We all need to dream. Babies dream more than old people, but even old people dream a lot. Dreaming may be important for brain cell formation, growth, and repair. It is important that you dream, which is why it is important to sleep.

## Waking Up in the Middle of the Night

Some phases of sleep are lighter, and for many people, between three or four in the morning is one of those phases. You wake up . . . your mind is flooded with ideas and you think, "I've got to do these things."

Your thoughts can sometimes be your enemy.

There you are, staring at the ceiling, thinking, "Don't forget . . ."

You can solve this with a pad of paper, a pencil, and a small penlight. Write down the thought because until you do, you'll keep cycling on it. "Don't forget to . . . this," and "Don't forget to . . . that." If you write it down, that completes a task. It closes the loop and then you don't think about it anymore.

You may say, "Yeah, but with what's in my head, I'd be writing all night."

Okay. Maybe you need to spend an hour writing down your thoughts. Then the next night it will be 45 minutes. Then the next night it will be a half hour, and the next, 15 minutes, and eventually you will work it out and write down all of the stuff that has been plaguing you. Because right now, you may be having two hours of interrupted sleep every night that affects your workday the next day. So it's worth writing it down.

There are also deeper phases of sleep when you just can't wake up. If you have ever taken a nap in the middle of the day that's a little too long and then felt exhausted the rest of the day, that's because you woke in the wrong phase of sleep. If you nap for about 20 minutes, that's probably about the right length so you won't wake up groggy and grumpy.

## A Soviet Psychologist Discovered What Is Keeping You Awake

A phenomenon called the Zeigarnik effect, named after the psychologist who originally made the observation, describes where the unclosed loops of thought that keep you up at night might be coming from.

Bluma Zeigarnik and several of her colleagues were having lunch at one of those nice restaurants where the waiters don't write anything down. Even though there were eight people around the table, the waiter recalled everyone's order perfectly. And the food delivery was just as magnificent.

They ate their food and left, and then (in an irony of ironies) one of the memory researchers in the party realized he had forgotten his wallet. So he, Zeigarnik, and some others walked back to talk with the waiter.

They said, "We were just over at that table and he forgot his wallet."

The waiter replied, "I'm so sorry about that. I'm afraid I don't remember."

"There were eight of us and I had the extra balsamic and he had the extra croutons."

The waiter once again said, "I'm sorry. I don't remember."

"You remembered our orders perfectly, and not 15 minutes later you can't remember who we are?"

He said, "As soon as you pay the bill . . . as soon as the check is closed, I forget everything that happened. It falls out of my head."

This is the Zeigarnik effect. Zeigarnik went on to design a series of experiments to study this phenomenon.

Imagine working on a project where you know all the numbers and you know all of the project details. However, as soon as the project is finalized and you wrap up all of the details, you can't remember anything about it. Out of sight, out of mind. Going back later to look at it, you see your handwriting in the file, yet you don't remember the people, the numbers, or the details.

Or how about this . . . you may recall a time in the days before contact lists and cell phones when you dialed a phone number over and over, trying to reach someone (and you'd get a busy signal?). Or a more modern example, you have to log in to an online account several times to fix an issue. After the first two times, you had the number or password memorized. However, as soon as the task was finished, the details faded away. That's the Zeigarnik effect.

The point here is that until you actually finish that project or finalize the details for a meeting, that information continues to roll around in your mind and can keep you awake at night. I call these "unclosed loops of thought." Rest comes when you close the loops. Writing down your preoccupying thoughts closes the loop, lets the thoughts all go out of your head, and then you can fall asleep.

## Aggressively Pursuing Unconsciousness

After electricity and all the distractions that came with it, the second enemy to good sleep is the digital alarm clock.

Because you wake up in the middle of the night and then you can't help yourself, you look at the clock . . . "Must . . . look . . . at . . . oh, it's 3:30 a.m. and I've got to get up at six. That means I've gotten two-and-a-half hours of sleep. I've got to go back to sleep . . ." Knowing what time it is gives you one more thing to worry about.

You turn your pillow over. You punch it. You put your head down and you say, "I must aggressively pursue unconsciousness. I must sleep." Then you can't help it . . . "Must . . . look . . . at . . . clock . . . It's 4 a.m."

You do not need to know what time it is in the middle of the night.

Here's a solution: move your alarm clock under the bed, in the drawer or across the room. If you've been awake for a while and you can't fall asleep, then just get up and go someplace quiet and write down what you need to remember.

If you have trouble sleeping, the bed is and should be reserved for two things—sleep and sex—and that's it. Not eating crackers. Not watching TV and not reading.

### The Lost Art of Rest

Both rest and recreation are important—but they are different things. You need time for doing nothing just as much as you need time to have fun. But when was the last time you did nothing? And, no, you can't include reading or watching TV—that's recreation or self-development, depending on what it is. I'm talking about sitting and doing absolutely nothing.

# People commonly confuse rest with recreation. Rest is doing nothing. Recreation is having fun.

Rest is sitting on your back porch with a glass of lemonade for two hours, watching the neighbor's kids play, watching the birds fly around. It's watching the waves come in at the beach or sitting in the woods listening to the wind play in the leaves. It's doing nothing.

Most Americans don't know how to do nothing. You may be thinking, "That would drive me crazy. I can't do that for five minutes." Well you might want to start for three minutes of doing nothing—or maybe one minute or maybe 30 seconds.

Time of quiet reflection is a time to slow and quiet your brain so you are able to think better.

## How to Rest Your Brain

Back in the "olden days" when everything was closed on Sunday, those really were boring days. There wasn't anything to do, and you know what? People had time to rest.

You need time for your brain to rest. The reality is that you may honestly feel you don't have time to sit down when you eat dinner—that's how busy your life may be.

I strongly encourage you to spend time doing nothing, and if you start out just doing nothing for one minute, that's good. And if you want music in the background . . . I said *nothing*.

This has been called "meditation," "contemplation," or, if you're from Oklahoma, "ponderin'," in years past. Today, it's trendier to call it "mindfulness." It actually is concentrated thinking on a certain task or on your current state—how you feel, where you are going.

It's not thinking about nothing. It's doing nothing and thinking deeply about something. It's not following your worries. It's thinking deeply about a topic or focusing your thinking on one thing.

If you practice yoga, you're taught to focus on your breathing. So to get started with this practice, learn to focus on one thing. To clear your head, begin by counting your breathing. When you breathe in and breathe out, count that as one. Breathe in and breath out again . . . that's two, and so on. You will find that your heart rate will slow and your blood pressure will decrease. At first, this may be challenging to do, but only because you have not been trained to do it.

This is not a religious tradition. There are people who meditate in various religious traditions, and they focus their thinking on one thing. The Christian mystics, the Jewish mystics, the Muslim mystics, the Hindu mystics, the Buddhist mystics, etc., all spent time concentrating and focusing. They had deeper thinking because they rested their brains.

## Sleep and Rest Life Success Story

Have you ever met an "idea machine"? One of those people who tends to be looking for new ideas? Ways to self-improve? Always learning and studying?

I have a great job because the people who hire me are excellent "idea" people and a blast to work with. One guy, Bill (not his real name), comes to mind—good looking, super-fit, set on money, physically active, and he has strong relationships with his family, a successful business, plenty of recreational time, and lots of friends. I like working with him. He applies the things I suggest, invests in himself and his business, and is generally making his life better.

Not long ago, Bill announced, "I recently did a sleep study. I found out I have sleep apnea and got a sleep machine. It is incredible! I have so much more energy. My thinking is so much faster and sharper. I had no idea what I was missing. They found out I was waking up 32 times an hour."

Bill looks nothing like the typical sleep apnea sufferer. He is lean, active, alert, mentally vigorous. He never complained of fatigue—in fact, people 10 years younger than him can't keep up—and yet, by taking care of his sleep, his vigor, alertness, and mental acuity were heightened. He's a great example of how even with success, with fine tuning, you can be even happier and more productive.

## Self-Assessment

How would you rate your Sleep and Rest Life?

---

Sleep and Rest Deprived                    Rested and Refreshed

1    2    3    4    5    6    7    8    9    10

---

Mark this page so you can transfer your score to the summary page at the end of the book.

You can also download the full evaluation of the Big 10 from DrRogerHall.com

*Regularly review how you are doing in all 10 areas. If you monitor them, you can manage them.*

## Steps to Improve Your Sleep and Rest Life

### Sleep Life Improvements

If your bed partner says you gasp in the middle of the night, you may have sleep apnea (when the soft palate at the back of your throat collapses). You will struggle to breathe—sometimes for as long at a couple minutes before you gasp. If your bed partner tells you this, get a sleep study done and look into either a breathing machine or a dental device to help open up your throat.

1.  Make sure your bedroom is dark. Nightlights tend to interrupt the sleep cycles of some people.

2.  Go to bed at about the same time each night and get up at the same time.

3.  Get a comfortable bed! Many sleep problems can be solved by a good mattress.

4.  Don't do anything but sleep and have sex in your bed.

5.  Don't overdrink or over-drug yourself in the evenings. Those chemicals will affect your sleep.

6. Don't exercise right before bed. The adrenaline could keep you awake.

## Rest Life Improvements

1. Spend time alone each day in quiet reflection—no music, no TV, no reading. Doing nothing.

2. Learn how to meditate. If you can't sit still, learn about walking meditation or find a local labyrinth to walk in. The monks in middle ages used them to walk and meditate at the same time.

3. Do less! We work on multitasking and being super-efficient. The happiest people have some down time for quiet reflection.

4. Go on a vacation where you don't see much, do much, or visit family. Lay on the beach or sit on a porch or in a hot tub, looking at the birds in the woods or on the beach.

# RECREATIONAL LIFE

*You need to have fun. If you're so focused on success and work that you never spend time with people you can have fun with, you're missing out.*

## Are You Having Fun Yet?

Recreation is about doing something that is fun. You may take vacations for rest—which is doing nothing—or for recreation. An example of recreation is going to Disney Land or Disney World. Depending on how you plan to do this and with whom, this may be a lot of work. Hopefully it will be fun too.

Recreation is supposed to be fun. If you don't have fun on a regular basis, you're missing out on a lot of life. So, you've got to figure out what's fun for you.

How do you schedule fun? Vacations come to mind. Have you taken a vacation in the last year? Was it fun? Or was it so overscheduled it was worse than an average workweek?

When I ask that question, I often hear, "No, it sucked. I spent it with my family." I was in a Hallmark store the other day and saw a card that read "Family" and on the inside read, "Will eat your soul." Of course, that depends on the family, but it's unfortunately true for some people.

**You need recreation and fun. If you're planning a trip that sounds less fun and more work than work, you might want to rethink that vacation.**

### The Los Angeles Lie

The last time you went on vacation, did you take your computer? Your phone? Did you let people from work call you?

When you allow work to call you or when you check your email on vacation, you tell yourself what I call the "Los Angeles lie." Have you ever been to Southern California? You may ask for directions: "I need to get from Santa Monica to La Brea, how long does it take?" If you ask anyone in Los Angeles, it doesn't matter how far away it actually is, they will tell you it takes about 20 minutes—depending on traffic. Yeah, that would be true by helicopter at one in the morning. But in real life, with traffic, that's a three-hour drive.

**You tell yourself the Los Angeles lie when you check your email on vacation.**

After the kids go to sleep, you're just sitting there, and what do you tell yourself? "Oh, this will only take 20 minutes to answer a couple of emails. I'll just knock those out." You end up sitting at your computer or on your phone until two in the morning, and then suddenly you realize you have a 6 a.m. breakfast with Tinkerbell.

That 20 minutes of emails took half the night. Now you're sleep deprived. You don't have uninterrupted fun. You don't have recreation. To have fun, you need to schedule time that is truly away from your daily details.

### Working Yourself to Death

How much vacation time do most employers give to employees in the United States?

Generally, it's about two weeks.

What is it in Europe? Depending on where you are, it can be anywhere from one to two *months* off. In Australia, it's two months.

In the United States, we take less vacation and less time for recreation and rest than most of the other countries in the world. (That's why we are the greatest country in the world.)

We also work more now than we worked 20 years ago. On average, Americans work 168 more hours every year than we did just 20 years ago—which is the equivalent, if we talk about 40-hour workweeks, of an additional work-month per year.

# In the U.S., there's no division between rest and work, or recreation and work. We don't have those natural limits.

Before cell phones and email, when you left work you would just get in your car and listen to the radio (or maybe your eight-track tapes). You would drive home. You'd rest. You would decompress and nobody would call you. Now we have these electronic leashes. People will text you and email you and call you at all hours of the day and night, which will interrupt the rest and recreation time you need, the relaxation time you need in order to be at peak mental functioning.

## Recreational Life Success Story

Do you have that one friend who is the "Renaissance Man" or "Renaissance Woman?" Most of us have one or two things we are good at, and then there are those people who, the more you learn about them, they are not only good, but great at a half a dozen things. I am not one of those people, but I do have one of those friends.

When I met Nick (not his real name), he was organizing a competitive rifle match. I showed up early as a participant, hoping not to embarrass myself by coming in last place. He had pulled up in his white pickup truck (the kind you see driven by people who work for landscaping and construction companies)—raggedy, dirty, the passenger side floor full of cardboard boxes, metal stakes, a staple gun, boxes of nails, and an assortment of loose tools. He went about his business setting up metal targets—some spun, some had levers which would drop down and pop up a clay pigeon into the air. Some had flappers that fell over. One was shaped like a star and when a target got knocked off the tip of a point, the star would spin—while the shooter was trying to hit the remaining targets on each of the other points of the star. I wondered where he bought all these things.

He went on stapling cardboard targets to long wooden sticks, stuck in wooden bases, making conversation about safety on the range and the rules for the competition.

When the rest of the guys showed up and the competition started, Nick and another guy were the "range officers"—it was their responsibility to make sure everyone was acting in a safe manner. I had him characterized in my mind as a helpful do-gooder. Then it was his turn to shoot. Holy mackerel! He was good! I can't remember exactly how it turned out that day, but he came in first or second place. I don't think I came in last, but not far from it.

Then I learned that not only was Nick a great shot, he had made all the metal targets and the complex contraptions. Over the course of months, I learned that he worked in a manufacturing facility that crafts railing (like the rails for your staircase or for a wrought-iron fence). Then he let it slip a few months later that he *owned* the railing company. Then he posted a couple of photos of some of his work. They weren't simply wrought iron rails; they were art.

Then I came to find out that Nick plays in a bar band with a couple of the other shooters. I imagined they must be small bars. Then I started seeing videos he posted. It didn't take long to learn that he's really good. Then several years later, he posted a video of a national television spot where he was playing with a national artist.

And he loves model trains (and for your information, so do Roger Daltrey, Rod Stewart, and Elton John).

I don't think the guy ever wastes time. If Nick isn't working to build beautiful iron art, he's tinkering around to make some new metal target contraption, shooting competitively at state and regional matches, practicing his keyboard, playing gigs, building artistic shelves for his daughter, or volunteering at the Christmas display of model trains.

And he is great at all these things! Moreover, he's having fun. How about you?

Successful people have enthusiasm. They love to invest their time in hobbies and activities that bring them pleasure. You may not, like me, have as many skills as my friend, but I am sure you have some skills you can have fun with. You can spend your time in diversion or you can spend your time recreating (re-creating yourself). And have some fun!

## Self-Assessment

How would you rate your Recreational Life?

---

| No Fun | | | | | | Regular Recreation and Fun | | | |
|---|---|---|---|---|---|---|---|---|---|
| 1 | 2 | 3 | 4 | 5 | 6 | 7 | 8 | 9 | 10 |

---

Mark this page so you can transfer your score to the summary page at the end of the book.

You can also download the full evaluation of the Big 10 from DrRogerHall.com

*Regularly review how you are doing in all 10 areas. If you monitor them, you can manage them.*

### How to Have Fun—Steps to Improve Your Recreational Life

1. I meet so many people who are so focused on self-improvement and making money that they never have any fun. That's not a successful life. You need to have fun. Successful people have fun—they don't just work. They laugh, they have fun, they get entertained.

2. How do you start having more fun? How do you be around people you have fun with? And if you don't know what's fun for you, you need to figure that out—what do you enjoy? When do you laugh? What do you look forward to, outside of work?

3. Ask your friends and family: When do you have a smile on your face or laugh out loud?

4. So, think about adding fun to your life—not just when you're on vacation, but during the workweek *and* on weekends. What that is will be different for everyone; it may be allowing yourself to play a silly game on your phone for 10 minutes or throwing a ball for the dog. Be deliberate about it.

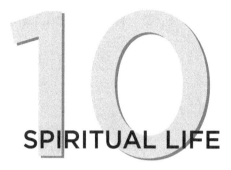

# SPIRITUAL LIFE

*Studies show that if you participate in a religious or faith community sharing common beliefs with others, you will be healthier and happier.*

**Statement of conflicting interests:** *I am a man of faith. What I am about to say supports my beliefs and worldview. I know it is hard, sometimes, to accept the word of someone who is rooting for his own team. Of course I'm biased. Knowing that, I'm still not irrational about my worldview. I'm not here to evangelize for any particular religion, but research done by people of faith as well as agnostics shows that people who are part of an organized religious community live longer, healthier, happier lives. In one report I read some time ago, it reported that religious people even have better sex lives. Which seems like a funny reason to get to know God . . . though His name comes up a lot.*

## The Good News and the Bad News

There's a great deal of research done in a number of major religions that shows people who share a religious belief and are actively engaged in a healthy faith community do live more satisfying lives.

# Research shows that people who share a religious belief and are actively engaged in a healthy faith community do live more satisfying lives.

Two researchers I respect, both agnostic, have reported that they know people of faith are more likely to be happy; but they themselves don't believe. As a result, they both said they need to work on the other areas of their lives in order to live life at its best. I'm not saying you need to be a part of my religion or even part of *any* religion. What I'm saying is that people I respect, who aren't on my "team," acknowledge that a faith life would help them have happier lives. If you can't make that intellectual leap, I get it. I'd suggest that you take their advice and make sure the other areas of your life are in tip-top shape in order to live a happier life.

## How Spiritual Growth and Participation in a Shared Faith Community Lead to Happiness

Alan Bergin was recognized for his contributions to the role of religious values in psychotherapy by the American Psychological Association in 1989, and he did a great deal of research on religiosity and health.

His work has been the basis for work by a number of researchers who have followed him. David Myers, Ed Diener, and others have looked at the relationship between religious involvement and happiness. In a 1995 study, the results were clear. Religiosity and well-being were well correlated. If you were religious, then you were likely to be happy. (Remember, correlation does not equal causation, nor does it indicate, if there is a causal link, which way it goes. It could be that happy people are more likely to become religious or that a third factor, like alien brain implants, could cause both religiosity and happiness—although unlikely.) In a more recent study, the results were a little less clear.

It seems that being a religious individual makes it more likely you will feel better, live longer, and be less likely to be a criminal. It seems that worldwide, living in a religious country is correlated to less happiness. Living in a religious state (in the U.S.) is correlated to less happiness and higher crime. So how is it that being religious helps the individual, but not the society?

It turns out that if you control for the wealth of the nation or the state, the negative effect of religion on society disappears. Poorer nations and states are more religious than richer ones. It is the lack of wealth that predicts unhappiness, short life, and crime, not religion.

David Myers summarizes a bunch of research in one of his papers and suggests that those who participate in religion tend to have these qualities:

- People who have the highest spiritual commitment are twice as likely to report being happy as the least spiritually committed (Gallup).

- Fifty-five percent of those "engaged" in a congregation are completely satisfied with their lives, while only 25 percent of those "actively disengaged" reported the same.

- The best predictors of well-being as an elderly person were health and religious commitment.

- Almost twice as many people who say they "feel God's presence" reported being happy than those who don't.

- Gallup also reported that religious Americans have higher well-being, less depression, and better health. They also reported that the more you go to religious services, the more positive and fewer negative emotions you feel.

- Being involved in a kibbutz (a strong Jewish community) predicts lower mortality (everybody dies, but it takes longer for it to happen if you have the protective effect of a strong religious community).

- In other studies outside of kibbutzes, it seems that religious involvement translates to an increased lifespan of eight years. It also translates to a much lower suicide rate. Nonreligious people have a seven times higher rate of suicide than the religious ones.

## The Good News and the Neutral News

In recent years, research results seem to blend together the concepts of "religiosity" (being involved in the practice of a faith) and the broader concept of "spirituality" (having awareness of a higher plane of existence and participating in spiritual, though not religious, activities). In some of these studies, since the ideas are blended, it is difficult to see how one is different than the other. If there is a difference, it could very well be that it is the presence of the faith community in one group, versus the more individualistic practice of the other. Perhaps the benefits of religion over spirituality, when found, are simply an effect of the social support network of the religious. That may be. While those who engage in spiritual practices outside of an organized religious tradition may benefit, often those benefits are solitary.

If you aren't religious but are spiritual, no doubt you gain benefit. It is hard to match the social support network that those in the body of faith experience from those who believe and practice in the same way.

Of course there are plenty of unhealthy and unhappy ways to practice one's faith. You only need to do a five-minute internet search to find troubling images of chuckleheads disrupting the funerals of veterans, yelling at people, and pointing fingers. What a relatively microscopic group of unhappy, angry people do makes for great news coverage. News crews typically don't show up to the thousands of houses of worship where people are preaching, praying, holding hands, and singing. Video footage of an older woman lovingly holding a fussy baby in the hallway outside the sanctuary so a young mother can sing, pray, and listen to a sermon in peace is way more boring than people with signs, spitting on others.

## Spiritual Life Success Story

People of faith who are financially successful are often misunderstood or suspected of faking it for the money. There is an old saying when speaking of religious missionaries becoming wealthy: "They came to do good, and did well." It is a snarky way to insult people of faith who have financial success—as if they hide under the cover of their faith to bilk others.

No doubt, there are those wolves in sheep's clothing. I've met them and I dislike them. It is inaccurate to lump all wealthy people of faith into that same category. One thing I've observed of the many, many people of faith who have had financial success: It isn't often because they pursued the money for the sake of the money. The financial success was a side effect of their priority of doing their job well. Doing their job well and in line with their faith-based values tends to breed financial success.

This was the experience of Paul (not his real name), one of my clients, although that wasn't evident for quite a while. Before he was a man of faith, Paul was in the relentless pursuit of money. He became an accountant, did his stint at a public accounting firm, became the CFO of a restaurant group, and in the midst of this aggressive pace, had a spiritual awakening. As is often the case, our real success comes from a series of bad decisions. Paul is no exception. In the midst of screwing up his life, he came to faith.

Unlike the movies, he didn't drop everything to go live in Africa to teach Pygmy kids to read. He knew business, he knew money, he knew restaurants, so he went back to work—but with a different purpose. Again, in a series of misfortunes (and maybe more bad decisions), Paul took over ownership of a struggling restaurant business. Struggling may be a little too optimistic a view of the shape of this business. It was upside down, bankrupt, in federal court, hounded by creditors, and pretty close to shutting its doors for good. As a chain of restaurants in a franchise, his business was not only under the microscope of outsiders, but also from the corporate giant. Everyone wanted their money, and if they couldn't get that, they might want a pound of his flesh.

In the time I've worked with him, Paul has (of course) had periods of frustration and anxiety, but the overarching mood I see in him is buoyant optimism—something he describes simply as "hope." He's a happy person. His business was tanking, but he wasn't. Over the course of our work, he slowly, laboriously dragged his business out of debt—all the while doing the delicate balancing act of figuring out how to pay the bills, keep the lights on, and serve customers in line with his values.

Paul's company is now out of the shadow of those days, profitable and expanding. It is a lot more fun to run the company now that many of the money and other issues are resolved, but neither the struggle nor the success has seemed to change him. He's almost always happy.

Paul's faith shaped the values that run his business: Hospitality—to the people who walk into one of his restaurants for a quick bite. Opportunity—for all of his employees—he wants them all to experience the opportunity to make their lives better. In spite of the rhetoric in the media of "corporate fat cats," I tend to find that business owners like Paul very often make decisions that are selfless. In his case, he has eaten the cost of some very expensive healthcare because a single one of his hundreds of employees has a vulnerable child. That employee will probably never know how much it is costing him to keep her employed. (He tells me she is worth it.) And he's happy to do it. He keeps going back to the values shaped by his faith and asks himself the question "What is the right thing to do?"

Paul is raising five kids, loving a few grandkids, and loving his wife. On the weekends, he plays violin at his church. Folks in the pew probably only see him as a musician. He doesn't seem to care. He's pretty happy in all of his pursuits and he credits that to his faith.

## Self-Assessment

How would you rate your Spiritual Life?

---

Not Part of My Life                                        Central and Regular

1      2      3      4      5      6      7      8      9      10

---

Mark this page so you can transfer your score to the summary page at the end of the book.

You can also download the full evaluation of the Big 10 from DrRogerHall.com

*Regularly review how you are doing in all 10 areas. If you monitor them, you can manage them.*

## Steps to Improve Your Spiritual Life

1.  Find a community of faith and attend.

2.  Make a personal devotional life a part of your daily existence.

3.  Volunteer and help others, alongside people of faith.

4.  Take a long hard look at the reasons you don't believe. If you can't reconcile yourself to a life with faith, work on the other nine parts of your life.

# OKAY, NOW WHAT?

I started this book with the quote from Tim Sanders: "Education without execution is just entertainment." As you are about to close the book, you are at a decision point. Do you check this book off your list of things to do as completed? Do you discuss the ideas with a friend or loved one over lunch? Do you tell yourself, and maybe your friends, that you could have done a better job writing this book? (Maybe you could have.)

None of that matters.

What matters is what one specific, behavioral action step are you going to take to improve your life today? (You can write that here if you'd like.)

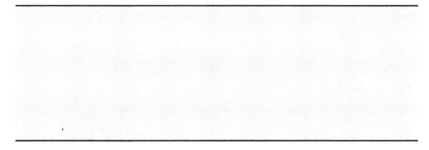

Having the knowledge contained in this book is good, but real success comes from actually doing something with it. You can have a stack of money stuck in the mattress and it will never grow. It only grows if you go out and invest it. The same is true with the knowledge contained in this book. How are you going to act to invest this knowledge into your life?

Choose one thing you are going to do **today** that will improve your life.

# Choose one area (and only one) as your starting point. What is the one habit you are going to change and make into your cornerstone habit of success?

Successful people don't just gather ideas and do nothing with them. Successful people act on their newfound knowledge. They start small, but at least they start acting. Imitate them and get their same success.

Now that you know the 10 important areas of your life to monitor, the next step is to evaluate yourself in these areas and rank them from 1 to 10. Then choose one near the bottom to identify that one thing you will work on and make a cornerstone habit for your future success.

Many driven and successful people have such full schedules they have to take a weekend away or a short vacation to find time for this kind of self-reflection. One friend suggested a three-day solitude retreat—seventy-two hours of time alone with no electronics and no human contact. Try it, if you never have. It could revolutionize your life.

Pick an area where you can get a quick win as your first step. Focus on that one area by setting a goal for improvement that you can measure.

Use the summary assessment of all 10 at the end of the book to keep track of your progress or download the form from DrRogerHall.com

When you achieve that goal, reevaluate your Big 10 and choose your next focus. It may take months to achieve that first goal, and it should.

## If it happens too fast, you won't have made it a habit.

I know, it's easier said than done. What took me a few short paragraphs to describe will take a lot of effort and time to achieve. Simple doesn't mean easy.

Take the assessment that follows to begin your next expedition into your growing success.

# THE **BIG 10** SUMMARY

You can download a PDF version of this evaluation at DrRogerHall.com

*Circle the number that best represents where you are in each of the Big 10 areas:*

1. How would you rate your thought life?

| Undisciplined Mess | | | | | | | | | Disciplined |
|---|---|---|---|---|---|---|---|---|---|
| 1 | 2 | 3 | 4 | 5 | 6 | 7 | 8 | 9 | 10 |

2. How would you rate your Exercise Life?

| Not a part of my life | | | | | | | | Regular and Vigorous | |
|---|---|---|---|---|---|---|---|---|---|
| 1 | 2 | 3 | 4 | 5 | 6 | 7 | 8 | 9 | 10 |

3. How would you rate your Nutritional Life?

| Not a part of my life | | | | | | | | Focused and Deliberate | |
|---|---|---|---|---|---|---|---|---|---|
| 1 | 2 | 3 | 4 | 5 | 6 | 7 | 8 | 9 | 10 |

4. How would you rate your Love Life?

| Awful | | | | | | | | Happy and Content | |
|---|---|---|---|---|---|---|---|---|---|
| 1 | 2 | 3 | 4 | 5 | 6 | 7 | 8 | 9 | 10 |

5. How would you rate your Social Life?

| Lonely and Isolated | | | | | | | | Strong and Enough | |
|---|---|---|---|---|---|---|---|---|---|
| 1 | 2 | 3 | 4 | 5 | 6 | 7 | 8 | 9 | 10 |

6. How would you rate your Work Life?

| Soul Crushing | | | | | | | Life Affirming and Meaningful | | |
|---|---|---|---|---|---|---|---|---|---|
| 1 | 2 | 3 | 4 | 5 | 6 | 7 | 8 | 9 | 10 |

7. How would you rate your Money Life?

| Money Problems (too much or too little) | | | | | | | Disciplined | | |
|---|---|---|---|---|---|---|---|---|---|
| 1 | 2 | 3 | 4 | 5 | 6 | 7 | 8 | 9 | 10 |

8. How would you rate your Sleep and Rest Life?

| Sleep and Rest Deprived | | | | | | | Rested and Refreshed | | |
|---|---|---|---|---|---|---|---|---|---|
| 1 | 2 | 3 | 4 | 5 | 6 | 7 | 8 | 9 | 10 |

9. How would you rate your Recreational Life?

| No Fun | | | | | | | Regular Recreation and Fun | | |
|---|---|---|---|---|---|---|---|---|---|
| 1 | 2 | 3 | 4 | 5 | 6 | 7 | 8 | 9 | 10 |

10. How would you rate your Spiritual Life?

| Not Part of My Life | | | | | | | Central and Regular | | |
|---|---|---|---|---|---|---|---|---|---|
| 1 | 2 | 3 | 4 | 5 | 6 | 7 | 8 | 9 | 10 |

Date: _____

Choose your first focus: _____

Six months later, reassess this: _____

# THE **BIG 10** SUMMARY

Use this duplicate for a re-evaluation in six months or download a PDF version of this evaluation at DrRogerHall.com

*Circle the number that best represents where you are in each of the Big 10 areas:*

1. How would you rate your thought life?

| Undisciplined Mess | | | | | | | | | Disciplined |
|---|---|---|---|---|---|---|---|---|---|
| 1 | 2 | 3 | 4 | 5 | 6 | 7 | 8 | 9 | 10 |

2. How would you rate your Exercise Life?

| Not a part of my life | | | | | | | | Regular and Vigorous | |
|---|---|---|---|---|---|---|---|---|---|
| 1 | 2 | 3 | 4 | 5 | 6 | 7 | 8 | 9 | 10 |

3. How would you rate your Nutritional Life?

| Not a part of my life | | | | | | | | Focused and Deliberate | |
|---|---|---|---|---|---|---|---|---|---|
| 1 | 2 | 3 | 4 | 5 | 6 | 7 | 8 | 9 | 10 |

4. How would you rate your Love Life?

| Awful | | | | | | | | Happy and Content | |
|---|---|---|---|---|---|---|---|---|---|
| 1 | 2 | 3 | 4 | 5 | 6 | 7 | 8 | 9 | 10 |

5. How would you rate your Social Life?

| Lonely and Isolated | | | | | | | | Strong and Enough | |
|---|---|---|---|---|---|---|---|---|---|
| 1 | 2 | 3 | 4 | 5 | 6 | 7 | 8 | 9 | 10 |

6. How would you rate your Work Life?

| Soul Crushing | | | | | | Life Affirming and Meaningful | | | |
|---|---|---|---|---|---|---|---|---|---|
| 1 | 2 | 3 | 4 | 5 | 6 | 7 | 8 | 9 | 10 |

7. How would you rate your Money Life?

| Money Problems (too much or too little) | | | | | | | Disciplined | | |
|---|---|---|---|---|---|---|---|---|---|
| 1 | 2 | 3 | 4 | 5 | 6 | 7 | 8 | 9 | 10 |

8. How would you rate your Sleep and Rest Life?

| Sleep and Rest Deprived | | | | | | Rested and Refreshed | | | |
|---|---|---|---|---|---|---|---|---|---|
| 1 | 2 | 3 | 4 | 5 | 6 | 7 | 8 | 9 | 10 |

9. How would you rate your Recreational Life?

| No Fun | | | | | | Regular Recreation and Fun | | | |
|---|---|---|---|---|---|---|---|---|---|
| 1 | 2 | 3 | 4 | 5 | 6 | 7 | 8 | 9 | 10 |

10. How would you rate your Spiritual Life?

| Not Part of My Life | | | | | | Central and Regular | | | |
|---|---|---|---|---|---|---|---|---|---|
| 1 | 2 | 3 | 4 | 5 | 6 | 7 | 8 | 9 | 10 |

Date: _____

Choose your *next* focus: _____

Six months later, reassess this: _____

# RESOURCES

**Listed below are some of the books, articles, and other resources I recommend for being happy and staying productive.**

Aslett, Don. *For Packrats Only: How to Clean Up, Clear Out, and Dejunk Your Life Forever* (March Creek Press, 2002).

Baumeister, Roy F., and John Tierney. *Willpower: Rediscovering the Greatest Human Strength* (Penguin Books, reprint edition, 2012).

Csikszentmihalyi, Mihaly. *Flow: The Psychology of the Optimal Experience* (Harper Perennial Modern Classics, 2008).

Dement, William. *The Promise of Sleep: A Pioneer in Sleep Medicine Explores the Vital Connection Between Health, Happiness, and a Good Night's Sleep* (Dell, 2000).

Mayer, Emeran. *The Mind-Gut Connection* (Harper Wave, reprint edition, 2018).

McKagan, Duff, and Chris Kornelis. *How to Be a Man (and Other Illusions)* (Da Capo Press, 2015).

Perlmutter, David, and Kristin Loberg. *Brain Maker* (Little, Brown and Company, 2015).

# END NOTES

1.  From a blog post by former NIMH (National Institute of Mental Health) Director Thomas Insel: https://www.nimh.nih.gov/about/directors/thomas-insel/blog/2011/antidepressants-a-complicated-picture.shtml

2.  Moncrieff, J., S. Wessely, R. Hardy. Active placebos versus antidepressants for depression. *Cochrane Database of Systematic Reviews,* 2004, Issue 1.

3.  Legrand, Fabien, Jean-Philippe Heuzé. Antidepressant Effects Associated With Different Exercise Conditions in Participants With Depression: A Pilot Study. *Journal of Sport and Exercise Psychology, Human Kinetics,* 2007, 29, pp. 348-364; Singh, Nalin A., Karen M. Clements, Maria A. Fiatarone Singh. The Efficacy of Exercise as a Long-term Antidepressant in Elderly Subjects: A Randomized, Controlled Trial. *The Journals of Gerontology: Series A*, 2001, Volume 56, Issue 8, 1 August, Pages M497–M504; Ernst, C., A. K. Olson, J. P. J. Pinel, R. W. Lam, and B. R. Christie. Antidepressant effects of exercise: Evidence for an adult-neurogenesis hypothesis? *Journal of Psychiatry & Neuroscience,* 2006, 31(2), 84-92.

4.  http://www.divorcestatistics.org/

5.  Imbens, Guido W., Donald B. Rubin, and Bruce I. Sacerdote. Estimating the Effect of Unearned Income on Labor Earnings, Savings, and Consumption: Evidence from a Survey of Lottery Players. *American Economic Review,* 2001, 91 (4): 778-794.

6.  http://fortune.com/2016/01/15/powerball-lottery-winners/

# APPENDIX:
# ALBERT ELLIS AND THE ABCS
# AN EXAMPLE

Albert Ellis was a great psychologist who came up with a way of remembering how to change your thinking and emotional reactions to adversity in your life by using the alphabet. I have expanded his theory a little, but it's his theory and I use it regularly for many of my clients, and it has worked wonders.

For ease of illustration, let's say my grandmother dies. That is the *Adversity* (or the *Activating* event)—the event in your life that knocks you for a loop. The death of a loved one, loss of a job, divorce—something stressful and life-changing and painful. What we think is the Adversity (my grandmother's death) causes the *Consequence*. Here's how we say it: My grandmother died. That makes me sad.

Here is where Ellis's ideas are so important. It is not the Adversity that causes the Consequence, it is our *Belief* about the Adversity.

My grandmother's death doesn't make me sad. It is my Belief about my grandmother's death that makes me sad. I believe that I'll miss her—I won't be able to call her up on Saturday morning and learn more about my grandfather. I'll never get another pair of socks from her for my birthday. I'll never get the apple walnut waffle recipe she promised to give me that was only stored in her head. I wish I would have told her I loved her one more time.

If those are the beliefs I have, then I will have the consequence of feeling sad. Adversity, Belief, Consequence.

Watch what happens when I change my belief: "Grandma's dead. Oh, good, now I get the money." The Adversity is the same, but my belief is fundamentally different. How do I feel? Happy? Change the belief, change the emotional consequence.

The Beliefs you have about the event or the person you lost are your interpretation of what it means to you now. Some of these may be irrational or inaccurate. Happy people tend to believe rational and accurate things. If you have irrational or inaccurate beliefs, you will have negative emotional consequences.

Being sad when my grandmother dies is neither irrational nor inaccurate, but it is uncomfortable. When we have uncomfortable emotions and especially when we have unpleasant emotions that are based on irrational or inaccurate beliefs, we become happier when we change our irrational or inaccurate beliefs.

C is for the emotional or behavioral Consequences of the Adversity. Some of these may be your reactions to the pain and loss and are a normal part of dealing with problems. However, when your beliefs are inaccurate or irrational, your thoughts drive negative emotional consequences that can become habitual and destructive, possibly to other areas of your life (job, relationships, etc.).

The D stands for four ways we deal with irrational or inaccurate thoughts and their unpleasant negative emotional Consequences.

The first D stands for *Denial.* (I'm not very good at Denial. I've met people who are *very* good at Denial. It is like they have a button in their heads that they push and they pretend and forget the unpleasant thoughts and emotions.) Let's use the Grandma example: Grandma dies, I think I'll miss her, I feel sad. Denial is the response, "Grandma isn't dead. I don't know why anyone would say that. She's just sleeping."

You're probably saying to yourself, "That is a whacked way of dealing with problems." Yes, it sure is. Denial is a negative short-term *and* a negative long-term way of dealing with problems. It is a pretty primitive way of dealing with problems and it usually doesn't work.

I know a man who needed to drive across two states to get to his wife and daughter (his daughter was very ill). He was staying with his parents. When he walked out to his car to drive to his wife and daughter, he looked at the gas gauge and realized he didn't have enough fuel to get there. He didn't have any money to buy gas, so how did he solve the problem?

He walked back into his parents' kitchen, took a box of cereal off the shelf, grabbed a pair of scissors from the drawer and a piece of tape. He cut a piece of cardboard from the cereal box, went back to his car and taped the cardboard over the fuel gauge. And started driving. This is NOT a typically proactive way to solve your problems, but people do it all the time.

The second D stands for *Distraction*. Distraction is very similar to Denial, but the person uses another activity to keep from thinking about the Adversity. Distraction is exceedingly common. It is a positive short-term strategy but a negative long-term strategy.

Let's go back to Grandma. Grandma dies, and I believe I'll miss her. I feel sad. (All normal and healthy here, but unpleasant.) I say, "I'm tired of feeling sad. I'm going to go to the movies and for two hours, I'm not going to think about Grandma." The movie is the Distraction. The movie is a good short-term, bad long-term strategy for dealing with unpleasant thoughts and emotions from an Adversity. It is also widely used. It's perfectly acceptable as a short-term relief from the unpleasant feelings. However, if after a year I'm still in the movie theater, it becomes destructive.

Distraction is the American way of life. Americans use Distraction as the way to solve every problem. Typically, we entertain ourselves in order to keep from thinking about our problems. We are an entertainment-soaked society.

After 9/11, we have hard evidence that people used Distraction to cope with the fear of the terrorist attacks. What is that hard evidence? Nine months later, there was a baby boomlet in New York. People Distracted themselves from their anxiety by having sex.

As I said, Distraction is a great short-term, lousy long-term strategy. If I need to keep going to the movies every day for a year to keep from thinking about Grandma, I have a problem. If New Yorkers refuse to get out of bed and keep having nothing but sex a year later, that may be a problem. The same is true for all Distractions. Bad day at work, want to relax with a beer? That is a fine short-term Distraction. Every day is a bad day at work? Transition from a beer to a 12 pack a day, every day, to Distract yourself from your lousy job; this is a lousy long-term strategy.

We can also use positive distractions. In order to avoid thinking about your lousy marriage, you focus on being the world's best soccer mom, baseball coach, or being the best at your job. All those Distractions are positive and productive, but they don't ever solve the problem of your lousy marriage.

The third D is *Deception*. Here I don't mean deceiving others, I mean deceiving ourselves. One of my presuppositions is that human beings are an inherently self-deceptive species. We lie to ourselves all the time. If we have an Adversity, we often lie to ourselves about the nature of it.

Let's look at Grandma: The obvious lie I could tell myself is this: "I never loved her. She smelled funny." That is an obvious lie, and not the kind we usually deal with when we respond to an Adversity. The more pernicious ones are lies that are mostly true. The best lies are mostly true.

"I miss Grandma (true). I don't think I'll ever be happy again (lie)." Those are the kinds of lies that get us into the most trouble.

What I find is that people who use Self-Deception as their default way of dealing with unpleasant thoughts and emotions tend to double down on their bad decisions. They become so adept at lying to themselves that they get themselves further and further in the hole. Our courtrooms are full of people who lie to themselves about situations only to be knocked in the head with reality when they end up in prison.

As you can probably guess, I think Deception is a lousy short-term and lousy long-term strategy.

The fourth D is *Disputation*. It is the only one that is both a positive short-term and a positive long-term strategy. It is telling myself the truth, based on *Evidence* (the E in this equation).

Grandma dies, I believe I'll miss her, I feel sad. When I Dispute with myself based on Evidence, I tell myself something like this: "I feel sad now and sometimes it feels like it won't end, but when I look at other people around me who have lost loved ones, and when I remember when I have lost other loved ones, I realize that we tend to go back to having a very good life. We still miss that loved one, but we go on to live productive, happy lives." So I know I will feel bad now while I am grieving, but it will get better.

What is the difference between Deception and Disputation? The quality of the Evidence. Bad Evidence is you are lying to yourself. Disputation is telling yourself the truth based on good Evidence. Remember: E is for the Evidence about your state of mind that results from questioning your beliefs and interpretations of the event. This involves clarifying your thinking about the event and finding alternative interpretations that can help you constructively move past the damaging consequences.

The final "E" is that you lead an *Examined* life, which is the life Socrates said is the only one worth living. If you Examine your beliefs, tell yourself the truth, argue against the wrong beliefs, don't deceive yourself, don't distract yourself excessively with entertainment and idle activities, and don't deny the difficulties in your life, you will lead a fulfilling, productive life. And it's only when you regularly and decidedly practice arguing with yourself about your wrong ideas that you will have an Examined, productive life.

# "The unexamined life is not worth living."

—Socrates

Ellis's model is a foundational way you can change your pattern of thinking. It requires that you slow down enough from Distraction to look for good Evidence to combat the irrational or inaccurate patterns of Belief that drive unpleasant emotional Consequences.

You may need help to learn to see the event in a new way, to challenge the inaccurate thinking. It requires questioning your reactions and conclusions about the event to find a new interpretation. You may need to enlist the help of a loved one, friend, or trusted advisor to help you get past your bad thinking habits and look for better Evidence.

# ACKNOWLEDGMENTS

Bev Newcomb and I have worked together since 1994. She was initially my secretary when I was employed by another organization. We both left that organization and a short time later, we started working together again. She has been a blessing to me every day of these years. For many years of my career, if anything was well produced or well organized, it was because of Bev. If there was a mistake, it was mine. In the now more than 24 years of working together, I'm pretty sure she has made only two mistakes in all of our work. She's kept me from looking like an idiot dozens, if not hundreds, of times. How does someone put together that kind of track record? This book was initially a speech I gave and recorded. Bev transcribed and edited that raw material so that we could have the basis of this book. Without her, this book would not exist, nor would much work that I hope you'll see in the future. She is a friend and I am grateful to know her and her husband, LH, who has been an advocate in my career.

Thank you to Kevin Harris and the Harris Harper Foundation for a seed grant years ago for a different book. Consider this the first fruits of your investment. There will be more. Thank you for your generous support those many years ago!

To the thousands of people who have heard me speak about the Big 10 for life success. Your feedback has helped me improve my message and encouraged me to spread it farther and wider.

To Maryanna Young, Jennifer Regner, and the team at Aloha Publishing— for believing in the project and shepherding it along the way.

Thanks to Keith York, for introducing me to Aloha Publishing.

To Brad Gibson, for 31 years of encouragement in the work I do and an example of success in life.

To Thom Leiter and Chad Dutka, for the creative headlines when this content was first put out as a blog.

To my casket carriers (the men who have walked beside me in adversity and helped me become a better man): Robb, Dan, Stan, Eric, Doug, and Chad.

To my wife, Patty, for her love, sharp mind, and sense of humor. I am grateful for you.

To my children, Sam, Luke, and Grace. You are never far from my thoughts and always in my heart, no matter where you may be.

To my sister, Laura, for the practical support in my work and life. It was hard to follow you through school. Still trying to measure up!

And finally, to my parents, George and Carol Hall, who will never read this book. You are the reason I have become anything. You made sacrifices, gave guidance, and provided the stability that made me the man I am today. I can never repay that debt. You will never understand how grateful I am.

# ABOUT THE AUTHOR

Dr. Roger Hall is a business psychologist and author with clients all over the country. He has one trick: he trains leaders to monitor and manage their thinking. Great leaders work on themselves first, and then success in their companies follows.

Roger received his Doctorate in Psychology from Ohio State University in 1991.

His clients are executives, professionals, and business owners. He helps leaders become better versions of themselves so they can lead their people better.

He has had the chance to consult and speak to all sorts of groups—from judges in federal courts, people in the intelligence community, company owners, executives, and university faculty, to social workers, teachers and nurses, construction workers, landscapers, and box-makers. He loves his work as a keynote speaker for financial services companies, judges, and technology companies.

He has worked with thousands of leaders—from Fortune 20 companies to small entrepreneurial firms. He is currently an executive coach for the Robert Wood Johnson Foundation Clinical Scholars program.

He and his wife, Patty, live outside Boise, Idaho, on the edge of the Boise National Forest where they look out their window down a canyon onto a hillside of pine trees. They traded the nighttime sounds of car alarms for elk bugling in their yard. They have a Labrador that doesn't retrieve and a cat that does. They have two horses that act like eight-year-old boys at recess.

He is grateful to be the father of three outstanding children: Sam, Luke, and Grace.

A great day for Roger includes jumping around on rocks in the mountains followed by an evening at the movies with a bucket of popcorn.

# LET'S CONNECT

Are you motivated to improve your life, your relationships, your work? Don't know where to start? I wrote this book to help you step back and examine your life using my Big 10 factors. Pick the one you feel will help you the most and let's connect on your action steps.

I would be happy to work with you individually or speak to your team or your organization.

If something in this book gave you an ah-ha moment, I would love to hear about it. I would be very grateful if you would be willing to post a review on Amazon.

Feel free to reach out to me through my website at DrRogerHall.com or email me at Hall@CompassConsultation.com or Roger@DrRogerHall.com.

Connect with Roger Hall on LinkedIn
Like @Compass Consultation, Ltd. on Facebook
Follow @Rogers2Cents on Twitter
Email Hall@CompassConsultation.com or Roger@DrRogerHall.com